Family Heaven
FAMILY HELL

Family Heaven Family Hell

HOW TO SURVIVE THE FAMILY GET-TOGETHER

Jo Ellen Grzyb

First published in 2007 by Fusion Press,
a division of Satin Publications Ltd
101 Southwark Street
London SE1 0JF
UK
info@visionpaperbacks.co.uk
www.visionpaperbacks.co.uk
Publisher: Sheena Dewan

A catalogue record for this book is available from the British Library.

ISBN: 978-1-905745-18-0

2 4 6 8 10 9 7 5 3 1

Cover and text design by ok?design
Printed and bound in the UK by
Mackays of Chatham Ltd, Chatham, Kent

For Fred –
Family Heaven because we're always working at it

Contents

Acknowledgements

First and foremost my biggest thanks go to Fred, who listened to every word as it was being written, went on his own personal journey and gave me lots and lots of suggestions, all of which I've used. I have huge gratitude to Leslie Gardner of Artellus Ltd for her faith in my work and words. Thanks also to Charlotte Cole, who had the initial idea for the book, and to Louise Coe, Kate Pollard and everyone else at Vision for seeing it through to the end.

Grenville and Elizabeth Clarke were willing guinea pigs for the early chapters and made excellent and useful suggestions. John Witt gave me loads of additional ideas and insights which have also been incorporated here. Lee McClelland gave me her keen eye and huge support. Impact Factory gets a nod for supporting all the time I took away from the company to squirrel myself away to finish the manuscript. A special thank you to Rose Youssef for her keen proofreading eyes.

Finally, I want to appreciate every friend, client and even casual acquaintance, all of whom opened their hearts to tell me their stories.

Introduction

Welcome to *Family Heaven, Family Hell.*

Here's what I can guarantee over the course of this book: I can guarantee some insight, some humour, some discomfort and some practical exercises for you to try out to help beat those family get-together blues.

I obviously don't know your particular family; you do. But I expect that by the end of this book you'll probably know yours a whole lot better than you do now. The better you know and understand how your family works, the better equipped you'll be to make changes in the way you behave when you're around them.

From my own experience and listening to the stories of others, I know that families can bring our greatest joys and our fiercest rages. When we get together with members of our families many deeply ingrained behaviours kick into gear, which turn the get-together into either a heavenly experience or a hellish one.

When I began telling people I was writing this book everyone but everyone had a reaction to the subject. Everyone had some kind of laugh – rueful, sarcastic, delighted, knowing, exasperated – and they all had some kind of comment to make:

'Oh, you should see my family!'

'I need to get a copy if I'm going to survive this Christmas.'

'I better buy one for my mother, who doesn't have the word "no" in her vocabulary.'

'You mean there *is* such a thing as family heaven?'

'Don't talk to me about families.'

'You can have mine if you want.'

And on rarer occasions:

'Birthdays are always great fun in my family.'

'I love getting together with our families; we never stop laughing.'

'I suppose every family can be hellish at times, but mine's all right.'

Whichever way you cut it though, the very topic created feelings in every person I spoke with, whether a new acquaintance or an old friend. Not only that, just mentioning the subject tended to open the floodgates of stories, sad tales, funny or horrible incidents, all filled with quite deep emotions. It certainly seemed to me that it didn't matter who I spoke to, what their age, gender, culture or religion, just the idea of the family get-together created strong feelings in people.

In the best of worlds, the family get-together can be a joyful experience. Unfortunately, a lot of us don't live in the best of worlds; we live in the real one. This is the one where family get-togethers can be a trying and unforgiving experience: our own personal family hell.

In this book I'll be exploring the dynamics of what happens when family members get together, the patterns that get repeated time and time again, the arguments that have been going on since time began (and before), the expectations, resentments and disappointments that get played out.

My intention is to help you identify your own roles in the family and how they continue to be perpetuated (I call myself the Human Buffer, but also, the Rebel With a Cause – more on this later). Everyone has two or three roles they play, and it's helpful to identify them so that they can be changed, if you so choose.

I want to show you that even in the most seemingly intractable situations, there are options. Often, when we're in the middle of an angst-ridden family event, it can feel as though there is no way out – that there aren't any options. We lose our ability to think and, therefore, to behave more creatively. I'll be providing you with lots of options to think about, try out and develop for yourself.

Reading *Family Heaven, Family Hell* will require some soul-searching, some courage and honesty, a whole lot of humour and a willingness for you to put your hand up to patterns of behaviour that might not put you in the best light. But the pay-off will be more tolerable (perhaps even fun) get-togethers, or the acceptance that now may be the time to walk away.

You don't need to examine why your families are difficult or unhappy, the important thing is to understand what happens and how it can be changed. I'm not interested in apportioning blame, uncovering deep, dark family secrets or unravelling jealousies. If you want to do that you probably need the professional support of a counsellor or therapist. The work of this book is about staying in the present and seeing what you can do *now*, at the very next family get-together, to make simple changes which will help you manage your own behaviour more effectively.

I have included quite a few case studies: some are personal to me; some are from families I have known for a long time; and some are the stories people have told me when I mentioned I was writing this book. In some cases, I've given people things to try out to see how they would get on with my suggestions, and their stories are woven throughout the book. All names (except my own and my husband's) have been changed and I have got permission from the narrators to use their stories.

How to use this book

Throughout the following chapters I'll be suggesting exercises for you to try out. You can do them anyway you want or not do them at all. You might want to write down or draw some of the feelings you experience as you read and use the exercises to chart your own progress as you go along. I encourage you to express your feelings as they arise.

One thing you might do is try some of the exercises with a trusted friend or even a member of your family. If you feel safe it's often easier to try out new things with someone else who's supportive and encouraging.

At the end of each chapter there will be a summary of things to be aware of, and things you can try.

1

Blood(y) Relations: Setting the Scene

We all come from a family

There's one thing that every human being on the face of the earth has in common: every single one of us has come from a family. It may be a loving and caring one or an abusive, rejecting one; you may be close to them or as distant as if they lived on the moon (even if they live right next door). You may have nothing much to do with yours, or not even know who your biological parents are, but somehow you did come from somewhere.

Families represent a bundle and turmoil of emotions we never really get away from. At worst, they 'run' us and we react to our families with little coherent thought; at best, we are surrounded by mature people who care about our welfare without trying to control it. There's a huge spectrum of behaviour between those extremes, and creating healthy relationships with our families is about moving out of the low end of the spectrum and getting closer to the high end.

How your family behaved towards you and what you have taken forward into your adult life will colour how you behave at family gatherings. Although this book is not about delving into how you got to be the way you are, it will be inevitable that some of the impact of your family history will be uncovered as you read each chapter.

Relatively speaking

What exactly is a family in this day and age? It certainly isn't Mum, Dad and 2.4 children, with a couple of sets of grandparents, sprinkled with an aunt and uncle or two and some cousins. Nowadays, it's Mum and her new husband and his children, parents and siblings. It's Dad and his live-in lover and her children, parents and siblings. It's Grandad on his third marriage, and Uncle James taking up a new religion and expecting everyone to be thrilled. It's single mothers and the occasional single father. It's gay sons and daughters more willing to come out than ever before. It's parents and grandparents who live longer but who no longer live with us. It's interracial and interfaith marriages. Cultures and languages intermingle in families as never before. Forget about the family tree; most of us have a mini forest of interconnections.

In my immediate family I have five siblings: an older sister from my father and mother and four from my father and stepmother. We have all been married at some point: eight marriages, the death of one husband, three divorces. Two of us have been married twice (me to the same person both times). My family is Jewish (me and my siblings are second-generation with grandparents from Russia and Lithuania), but we've married people who are Jewish-Catholic, Muslim, Catholic and Methodist. Spouses have included two second-generation Poles, a native-born Moroccan, a second-generation Irish, a native-born Chinese and one whose American family stretches way back. Two of my siblings have two children each; one has three; the remaining three (I'm one of them) have chosen not to have children. We were all born and brought up in or near Boston, Massachusetts (the USA one). Here's where we all live now: England, Rhode Island, Alaska, Minnesota, Texas and, amazingly, Massachussetts. Every single one of us has a career.

That's quite a cocktail and I expect is very different from what our grandparents might have expected of their grandchildren.

It's not like it used to be

The whole nature of families has changed radically over the past few decades and, therefore, our expectations and beliefs around how they and we should behave within them is beyond recognition to how families behaved 50 years ago.

In the West certainly, the reality of families changed fundamentally during the First World War and even more radically from the Second World War. Up till then, roles in the family were mostly clear-cut: father worked, mother bred and brought up the children. Children were expected to look after their parents in old age. Whether they liked it or not, most couples stayed together as divorce was rare and extremely difficult and primarily available for the upper-middle and upper classes. A family hierarchy existed that still had a foot in the Victorian era, where children were seen and not heard (and often not even seen), father ruled the roost and if mother did work, it was certainly rarely the equal of men and usually of necessity rather than choice. Not only that, people tended to stay where their families were and villages and towns had generations of families buried in the local cemeteries.

A lot has changed. My long-deceased grandparents would not be able to recognise the lives I and my siblings and their children lead today. The way we marry, give birth and die can be a million miles away from two or three generations ago. Weddings on the tops of mountains and barefoot on beaches? Civil ceremonies for gay couples? Increasing numbers of marriages sanctioned by the state instead of by religion? Births in hospitals, in tubs of water, with fathers assisting, without fathers at all? IVF, middle-aged pregnancies? Birth control, abortions, one-child families, no-child families?

The First World War changed the social fabric of the way we in the West deal with death. Before the war, people were involved in the death of loved ones and shared grief helped people mourn. During the war to end all wars, the youth of many countries died far away and families were told by letter and later by telegram. In many cases there was no body to bury. A whole generation was first overwhelmed and then numbed by the sheer number of deaths and the distance from their loved ones.

Wars continue to have that additional psychological impact today. Even without wars, we seem to have distanced ourselves from the process of death with more and more people dying in hospital instead of at home.

Three of the big family events – marriage, birth and death – no longer look the same, and then there are other social and economic influences to factor in to our ever-changing culture.

These days, in every strata of society, there's a good chance that both parents have jobs, divorce has exponentially increased since the Second World War (though there are indications that the divorce rate is currently declining), people move away, take jobs overseas, study abroad. People cohabit as a matter of course, have children out of wedlock or don't have any at all. Vastly fewer women die in childbirth and many diseases have been completely eradicated. Birth control is readily available and routinely practised, even by people whose religions don't sanction it.

I've just been talking about the West but, in many other parts of the world, the notion of family is changing as well. Even in societies and cultures that have a more rigid hierarchy than that which is currently the norm in the West, families are evolving. Divorce and cohabitation rates may not be as high as in the West (though in countries like China they're gaining fast); gay children may keep their homosexuality more hidden in some cultures than in others; fewer children may be born to single mothers; and, in many parts of the world, mortality rates among mothers and infants are still high – many diseases wiped out in the West still kill hundreds of thousands elsewhere. However, nearly every society in the world is being affected by the bigger socio-economic changes happening around the globe.

But wherever you go in the world, if you strip out that which makes us different, family still exists. It is family that is universal and is our common ground. Take away the trainers, chadors, dugout canoes, crucifixes, saris, turbans, muumuus, iPods, bikinis, snowshoes; take away religions, skin colours, races; take away English and Italian and Arabic and Swahili: it is the family that persists.

Now this book isn't an exploration of divorce rates or societal 'revolutions' but it is interesting to note that, as the structure of families change everywhere you go, so will the family get-togethers become a different 'animal'.

Case study: Violet's story

Violet is an 83-year-old widow living on her own in a small town in Cumbria. She has three children, five grandchildren and two great-grandchildren.

'I was 19 when I got in the family way and it was impossible to get married to the father. I was terrified and panicked and when my parents eventually found out I was sent away as soon as I began to show (they told people I was a land girl and was somewhere in Somerset). As soon as the baby was born it was taken away and I returned home.

'No one ever said a word about what had taken place; and my parents pretended nothing had happened. They wouldn't speak to me or even look at me directly for nearly six months. I pretended as well. I did eventually marry, to the relief of my parents and my husband never knew either. I've carried around grief and shame, loss and anger my whole life.

'One of my grandchildren, Elise, has a son. She's what they call a single mother these days; there's no father around as far as I can tell. When she came home from hospital there was a big party to welcome Sam into the family. Everyone was there and I had such a mix of feelings I was nearly overwhelmed.

'I was amazed that everyone, every single person in the family, seemed to think it was normal. Having no father around was normal! They were just happy Sam and Elise were healthy.

'More than my amazement, I am reluctant to confess, I was jealous. I'm still jealous, even though I love them both and she's so good bringing him round to see me every week. I'm jealous of how easy Elise seems to be with being an unwed mother. I'm jealous she has her son when I didn't even know the sex of my baby. I'm jealous that Elise's parents – my daughter and son-in-law – haven't condemned her or made her feel ashamed.

'I'm happy for her, don't get me wrong. But I think of all the lost years without my child and it's all so different now.'

It's true that many things we take for granted now were extremely rare except in the most accepting of families. Indeed, many of the tensions that exist within families are caused by the changes our society is undergoing that, in a sense, give permission for behaviour unheard of by our grandparents.

Although many family get-togethers have been hellish since families began, a major difference from half a century ago (or even more recently) is the desire and willingness to challenge the status quo. 'Respect your elders' meant accepting their behaviour, whatever it was. It didn't matter if it was autocratic, bullying, drunken, boorish, embarrassing, people put up with it because that was the norm. In a rigidly patriarchal culture, generally the word of the head of the household is 'law'. People may not have liked it, but they didn't question things the way we do now. The norm has changed out of all recognition.

The culture we live in at present encourages people to change what they don't like.

Cultures are continually shifting so who knows what it will all look like in another 50 years' time, but right now we live in a climate that says it's good to try to make the family get-together more enjoyable. It's OK to look at survival tactics rather than enduring the unacceptable.

There are still plenty of rigidly dictatorial families out there, and there are plenty of people who still endure the unacceptable because they don't have the understanding, skills, courage or willingness to take the necessary steps to make needed changes. In many cultures, too, it can even be dangerous to question the status quo, let alone act outside of it.

People have always longed for love, acceptance and nurturing from their families, but not necessarily with any expectation that they might or even should receive them. We still long for those same things but now we have a far stronger belief that we should be given love and acceptance from our families; we demand it, we fight about it, we are frustrated, hurt and angry when we don't get it.

My mother's generation (she's 89 now) may have hoped like hell for their families to be pleasant and caring when getting together, but I doubt it would have occurred to most people a few decades ago that there was much they could do to change the family dynamics. Our society has changed so much that now we not only desire the changes, we believe we deserve them and that we can instigate them as well.

I do not want to put too fine a point on this, but it takes courage – vast reservoirs of it – to change the status quo, even if our current culture gives us tacit permission to do so. Our blood ties and the patterns with which we have developed will often still be stronger than our capacity to change them.

My intention is that the small, doable steps I will offer for your consideration will help you gain that courage.

What's in your cocktail?

It's important to look at your own cocktail and see just what the 'mix' is in your family. I do know that in quite a few families the more people who are added to the 'mix', the more difficult it can be to deal with family issues: they just get compounded. There are many more opportunities for tension, disagreements, culture clashes and differences of opinion.

Case study: Christine's story

Christine, 34, works as a receptionist in a dental practice in Liverpool. She comes from a small family and thought they were relatively close.

'What has happened to my family? Everything was fine, mostly, till my baby sister Lisa married the bloke she's been living with for a year. Something changed and Geoff started to push his weight around and get very bossy.

'Suddenly it's like we're all arguing every time we meet up. Before then, we didn't argue so much. We didn't always get along, but we kind of kept a lid on things. Now it's like the lid's off and we're at each other's throats all the time.

'My sister keeps saying we're taking sides against Geoff, and she's probably right. But it's like we're fighting with each other and no one ever says anything right to his face.'

What's most interesting about Christine's story is that it didn't take a lot to upset the delicate balance at her family get-togethers. It can be very tricky introducing someone new into the family mix. In Christine's case, her brother-in-law Geoff had been around for a while, but as soon as he became an 'official' member of the family it all changed.

Whether good or bad, when we grow up in our families, we get to know and even to predict how most of our family members are going to behave. It's unusual for someone to spring completely unexpected and surprising behaviour on us, unless that's one of their roles in the family (more on roles in Chapter Four). We get used to someone always being the peacemaker or the drama queen or the gossip. We may not like it, but other family members' behaviour becomes very familiar over the years.

Not only that, we all have a shared history. We have short cuts in the way we talk to each other and family 'jargon'; we have 'signals' that everyone understands and, of course, in many families there are secrets that people outside the family know nothing about.

Drop someone new into the blend and it can all become something very different from what we're used to. In Christine's story, just one new family member upset the status quo and their get-togethers began moving into hellish territory.

Maybe you have a family that's always made the get-together hard going. Maybe you have a family like Christine's that got along well enough until someone new came into the mix. Perhaps just the opposite – someone new entered the family and your relatives suddenly started behaving themselves. Maybe you have a family where there are little factions, where some people get on with one bunch but not with another.

Let's take a look at your family members. Do you have a large 'nuclear' family – one linked by blood ties? Do you have more of an extended family, with gangs of people coming from the 'outside'?

Exercise one

What's your mix?

If your family cocktail is made up of as many different ingredients as mine is, take a few minutes to list them. If your cocktail has just a few, list them as well.

My cocktail ingredients are:

____

____

____

Now take a note of who does or doesn't get along with whom.

Who gets on with whom?	Who doesn't?

I'll be looking in-depth as the book unfolds at exactly what happens in your family, but for the moment, just see if you can identify where the 'mix' works and where it doesn't.

In my family, for instance, we siblings are more likely to have a go at each other than at anyone from 'outside'. Actually, overall I think we're pretty good at welcoming new people in. It's not the new mix that's the problem, it's the old one.

Great expectations

Family difficulties have existed as long as families have, but we now expect different things from our families and it's often those expectations that can make or break the family get-together.

There's nothing wrong with having expectations, but too often we'll hope that if someone else would just change their behaviour, then things would be a whole lot better. I expect most of you will have an image of how you want your family to behave that would make the family get-together more bearable.

Here are some of the things people have said to me:

'I wish my mother would really listen to me.'

'If only my brothers weren't so competitive; they always spoil things for everyone else.'

'Life would be much easier if we didn't bicker all the time.'

'My sister is a real prima donna and expects to get her own way with everything.'

'My stepmother is an empty-headed idiot who only thinks about shopping and only talks about sales.'

'My parents never tell me they're proud of me.'

'My uncle has a drink problem and ruins every family party we ever have.'

All these wishes are clearly heartfelt, but do you notice how they're all about someone else needing to change. In all the chats I had I don't think I heard more than a couple of people accept any responsibility for what may go wrong at their family gatherings.

So the expectations are high and at the same time it's everyone else who has to change in order to meet those expectations. Much more on this later.

Another common thing that happens in families is that no one tells anyone else about what they wish could be different;

those wishes stay hidden in people's minds with the assumption that the other person/people will know exactly what's wanted.

Here's a good example of what I mean:

Case study: Silvio's story

Silvio is a 43-year-old Portuguese construction worker living in Faro with his wife, Amalia, and their two children. He has two older siblings, a brother and a sister, both of whom have children as well.

'When Amalia and I got married, we argued about it but eventually agreed that she'd keep her job even when we had children. My parents had helped my brother and sister when they first had children, babysitting, helping with meals, so of course I assumed that when I had kids, they'd offer the same help to me.

'Except it didn't happen that way. We had our first, Alberto, and everyone was as excited as if he'd been the first grandchild. I waited for the offers of help, particularly as Amalia planned to go back to work part-time after four months.

'No offers came. Not once. Not even to babysit so we could go to the cinema. I became really jealous of my brother and sister, even going as far as resenting my nieces and nephews because they had got my parents' attention while Alberto wasn't getting anything.

'Every time they came over cooing at the baby I fumed inside, "If you think he's so cute, why don't you offer to take care of him every once in a while?" It got so bad I couldn't look at them and I got really nasty at times till we finally had a big argument over who Alberto's godparents were going to be. There was no way I was going to ask my brother and his wife, which is what everyone expected.'

All that chatter in Silvio's head. He's now created a family rift that may or may not have any basis in reality. Because he's kept his thoughts and expectations to himself ('They ought to offer') no one really knew how deep his feelings were. I'll be retuning to Silvio's story later in the book.

What are *your* expectations? Like everyone else, you will have expectations of your family. As I give you more examples throughout the book, you may be able to identify others, but for now, see if you can list any expectations you have when getting together with your family.

My great expectations are:

____

____

____

____

____

One friend I spoke to said when she gets together with her three sisters her great expectation is, 'That no one gets hurt.' That tells you a lot about what usually goes on at those gatherings.

I'm not asking you to do anything with your expectations at the moment, but when you think about them or write them down, how do you feel about them?

Coming together

I've touched a bit on the family; now it's time to look at the family get-together.

We come together to celebrate, mourn, congratulate, observe, honour, remember, acknowledge. Families have an endless array of get-togethers to choose from where they can enjoy, take delight and appreciate each other . . . or not. There are events when we can either have a terrific time with our relatives or we can make ourselves and others truly miserable.

There are birthdays, anniversaries, religious holidays, funerals, Sunday lunches, christenings, summer barbecues, weddings, picnics, trips/holidays, hidden agenda visits, meet the in-laws, retirement parties, elder parent decision-making meetings, naming days, reunions, surprise drop ins. There are intimate gatherings or crowds big enough to get lost in. Family get-togethers can include eating, drinking, dancing, walking, talking, embracing, crying.

I had one of the best family get-togethers – if not *the* best – about 15 or so years ago. It was the Fisher family reunion – a proper family reunion on my maternal side. Myriads of cousins, second cousins, eighth cousins five times removed. There was dancing and singing and a video someone had transferred from cine-film of the patriarch of the family (my great-grandfather) when he first came to America. This was the kind of family get-together that was truly heavenly: I caught up with my favourite cousins; had fun with my mother, older sister Beth and my two nieces, Kelly and Erin. I danced till my feet ached. It was probably the first time in my whole life I got a feeling of really being part of a massive family, most of whose members I'll probably never see again.

I had been to a couple of these reunions when I was younger, but their significance didn't make any impression. This time it did.

That's my benchmark for a good time with the family.

Exercise two

What's yours?

My best family get-together was:

____

____

____

____

____

That's about the best, what about the worst?

Family get-togethers can also include arguments, yelling, storming off, frustration, annoyance and silent suffering.

I'll be talking about one of my worst further on in the book (you'll know it when you get to it), so for the time being, see if you can identify the worst family get-together you've had.

My worst family get-together was:

____

____

____

____

____

We come together to be with people we haven't seen in years or months or just days. There is something about coming together with members of our family that *should* make us feel loved and cared about and nurtured. Only too often just the opposite happens and we go away from these gatherings feeling aggrieved, frustrated, rejected or depressed, with our hopes and expectations ending up in disappointment.

What lies beneath

Every family event will have an obvious purpose (wedding, christening, bris, summer barbecue, retirement party) and on the surface that's why people gather. But other issues are often at play at the same time. These are the ones that never seem to go away or get resolved.

As this book unfolds, I'll be looking in detail at the many differences between family heaven and family hell, and there are many. It's not all sunshine and roses in family heaven, where everyone loves and respects each other and no cross words are ever spoken. Don't we just wish.

But family heaven can and does exist, just not in the form that many people imagine. When in the midst of family hell, it seems easier to fantasise that other families get on so much better, have a happier time and are pretty much perfect. This way people get to dismiss their own difficult families as hopeless and look to these imagined 'perfect' families as wonderful. It's easier to do that than to accept that there are no perfect families; that even in the best of them, there are difficulties: sibling rivalries, favouritism, unhealed hurts.

When we look at what lies beneath, it's the hidden agendas and unfulfilled yearnings that can blight even the happiest get-together.

We're often looking for proof of our family's love for us. We wrap up our desires in less obvious ways (for example, in Silvio's situation love=babysitting), but in general it's safe to say that many of the arguments, resentments, jealousies, hurts and frustrations stem from feeling that we aren't loved in the ways we need. That is our greatest expectation: that when we get together with our families we will be loved in the ways we need to be loved, which is not necessarily how we are actually loved by others.

With all that sitting within us, usually unexpressed, it's no wonder there's friction. Again, this is something I'll be looking at in far more depth later in the book, but I just want to flag up for now that family get-togethers are far more complex events than whatever it is that's drawing people together.

In family heaven, people really get to enjoy the actual event: the wedding, Sunday lunch, bar mitzvah, birthday party or whatever celebration or sadness that has brought people together. The heavenly family takes joy and comfort in being together whether it's for a wedding or a funeral. Remember, these aren't perfect families, but they are people who get beyond the petty squabbles which trap hellish families in repeating unhelpful and often painful patterns.

In family hell, the event is often secondary to whatever is being played out amongst the family members.

Case study: Anna's story

Anna is 26, a newly qualified solicitor at a Leeds law firm. She is straight-talking when she's at work, but finds herself becoming Miss Jelly when she's with her older brother.

'I can laugh about it now but at the time, I was completely horrified. It was my father's funeral and I was there with my mother, my aunt (Dad's sister), my two brothers and their wives and children. Plus all my dad's friends from work and the neighbourhood – he was very popular.

'We got through the service and I thought, "Well at least we're not fighting," which is kind of sad that that's what was in my mind. There we were saying goodbye to my father and I was relieved we weren't bickering.

'The trouble started when we went to get into the limousines which were taking us to the cemetery: we had to decide who was going to sit in the lead car. Being the ever-hopeful peacemaker, I said, "I'm fine, I really don't mind which car I go in." My older brother insisted that it had to be Mother and the three of us children. My younger brother wanted to be with his wife and my aunt was clinging so hard to my mother that I thought it would have been impossible to prise her off.

'This was all being done in whispered hisses while everyone else stood around, embarrassed, looking at the ground, waiting to follow the hearse.

'If it had just been the stress of the funeral I probably would have been able to forgive my brothers, but this one-upmanship had been going on for as long as I could remember and it was clear it wasn't going to stop just because my father had died.

'By this point I was in floods of tears, not for my father, but out of sheer frustration that not even his death made any difference.'

We can see here how the event of Anna's father's funeral became less important than the age-old patterns that Anna and her family were used to playing out. Even in the midst of sadness it can be almost impossible for some families to step outside their patterns and behave differently.

Even in the midst of happiness that can happen as well.

Case study: Steven's story

Steven is 32, from a farming family in the Midlands, with a very large extended family.

'I was the last of my three brothers to get married. My parents were worried I'd leave it too late, so they were thrilled when I announced my engagement. They decided to pull out all the stops for the groom's dinner. I'm not a great one for parties but I was happy to go along with it all and my future wife, Rachel, thought it was sweet, all the effort they were going to.

'That is, until it came to the dinner itself. Everything seemed to be going really well. The pub was great, the food was good, I was even beginning to enjoy myself and relax as nothing had gone wrong. I didn't even drink too much to get relaxed.

'I couldn't even tell you what happened but, sitting with Rachel's family, I started hearing my parents argue. "Oh damn," I thought, "not tonight."

'I fell over myself to get over to their table to see what was wrong. My brothers had the same idea and we all got there as Mum and Dad were getting louder and louder. They didn't seem concerned that they were in the middle of a crowd and causing a scene.

'This wasn't new. We'd all been here before. I really had hoped that that night, when we were all having such a good time, they'd behave themselves.

'No such luck.'

In both scenarios, some of the family members just couldn't get beyond their own emotions for the sake of the rest. When something like that happens, other family members usually get caught up in the inappropriate behaviour and the cycle of patterns gets repeated.

It would be easy to condemn families like these to the scrap heap of hopelessness. When we are in the midst of our family's embarrassing, appalling or rude behaviour, it's easy to dismiss them as useless.

They're not.

If it was completely hopeless you wouldn't have bought this book. If your family was completely useless you wouldn't bother. You have hope that something could change to make your family gatherings better.

Are heavenly families so different?

Case study: Johnson's story

Johnson is a 45-year-old oncology lab technician, living and working in London. He's married with two children: a son and a daughter.

'I think my family's kind of normal with the normal ups and downs of family life. We've been through some tough times – mostly to do with things outside our control, outside the family – and that's brought us all a lot closer over the years.

'Most of us live in the same neighbourhood; my parents are right around the corner.

'Family parties are our favourite times. There's food, of course, and we laugh like drains. My younger brothers and I have a quiet rivalry we've kept going: who's got the better job, who got married first, who had the first grandchild, who brings Ma and Pa the best gifts. It's harmless and is now more a family joke than anything serious.

'The worst family fight came at my son's seventh birthday party – another good excuse for a big party with Luke's friends and the whole family. When Luke was opening his pile of presents, my father announced his gift: he had arranged for Luke to go back to Jamaica to go to the best school in St Ann's Bay.

'My wife, Jamilla and I were speechless, but not for long. Luke started to cry and I blew my top. "How could you do that? How dare you make a decision like that without even consulting us? Who's business is it where Luke goes to school? Certainly not yours."

'Ma and Pa were really upset, Luke's friends all wanted to know when he was leaving and his sister, Sophie, was crying too. "Why aren't I going? Why does Luke get to go away and not me?"

'What a fiasco. It took me a couple of days to calm down as I wasn't talking to my parents; Luke and Sophie weren't talking to me; and Jamilla and I had long talks about what to do.

'I finally went over to speak to them. It took me a while to realise that they were only doing what they had done when I was seven. They had sent me back to Jamaica to school and to live with my auntie Marianne. They hadn't been in Great Britain all that long and their connections to "home" were very strong. I was born in London but they talked so much about St Ann's that I felt I knew it. Going back there to school seemed very normal; lots of families did it.

'I had to explain to them how much times had changed, that sending me back seemed the right thing to do when I was a kid, but Jamilla and I just weren't going to be parted from Luke – we were a family and we needed to stay together. I had to do this without making them think that what they had done to me was wrong, because it wasn't. But Luke wasn't going to St Ann's. I decided (thanks to Jamilla's wise counsel) not to even mention how angry I was that they made this arrangement without even talking it over with us. Jamilla said that would be a red herring – the more important point was to let them know our decision without hurting them more than they already were.

'It took more than one conversation because not only were they hurt but they felt I shamed them in front of the rest of the family. I had turned down their gift and I had lost my temper. Whether I was justified or not wasn't the issue. Getting us talking and healing the breach was what was important.'

Everything that happened to Johnson and his family can happen to any family: an unexpected piece of news, an emotional blow-up and the fallout from it all. In this heavenly family, however, the effort wasn't directed at who did what and who was wrong, but on how to get the family back on an even keel. It also took an understanding of what was behind it all instead of focusing on the 'how could you?'

I'll be looking at heavenly families in a lot more detail later on in this book, but Johnson's story is to illustrate that heavenly families have just as hard a time as anyone else; it's how they deal with those hard times that sets them apart.

Big events, big feelings

Ever notice how sometimes the big family dramas tend to happen during the really important get-togethers such as Christmas, Thanksgiving, Diwali, Eid ul-Fitr, Bon Festival, Rosh Hashana, New Year's Eve, etc? These aren't just family events, they represent something larger which has to do with people's religions, country cultures and national traditions.

Wherever they are in the world, it's as though people store up their crises so they happen right in the middle of one of these big family get-togethers. Couples announce they're splitting up, secrets get revealed, explosive arguments burst out of seemingly nowhere. More than at other times, it seems as though someone invariably gets drunk or soppy or abusive. Lots of people told me stories about big fights, hysterical scenes, smouldering angers that all came to a head during what was supposed to be a good time. Tensions often seem to be at their highest when you combine a family event with a big religious or national event.

The messy stuff seems to emerge tenfold when the 'festive' spirit – whatever the festive time – is supposed to be around. Expectations are higher around big holidays; no matter where you go there are images in every culture that show happy families and joyous times during these special days of the year.

Not only that, the big holidays are often times when people who don't see each other for the rest of the year come together and are supposed to get on with each other. Sometimes that happens and people are delighted to come together, get up to date with each other's lives and so on. Sometimes just the opposite happens and age-old hurts and resentments that have been festering flare up because the lead players are on stage with each other once more.

Before I get on to the things you can to do to start making it better, however, you do have to unpick what actually happens in your family that makes it more hellish than heavenly.

The hell to heaven scale: the good, the bad and the downright ugly

I think of family get-togethers on a scale of 1 to 10: disastrous (1) through to jolly good fun (10).

If I look back to say, celebrating Passover with my mother and older sister, my mother's parents, one of my aunt and uncles and four of my cousins, those events definitely rate a 10. My normally remote grandparents seemed to really enjoy having us around and they were more relaxed than normal. There was always laughter and games and my grandfather would challenge us to wicked bouts of Scrabble where he gave no quarter. Whereas, it's safe to say that some of my family gatherings with all my siblings in one room might score a 3; not a complete disaster, but close.

What about you?

Exercise three

Part I

Try filling this chart out as honestly as possible.

Event	Who was there	Hell to heaven scale
1.		1-2-3-4-5-6-7-8-9-10
2.		1-2-3-4-5-6-7-8-9-10
3.		1-2-3-4-5-6-7-8-9-10
4.		1-2-3-4-5-6-7-8-9-10
5.		1-2-3-4-5-6-7-8-9-10

For some of you it may very well be that you can't identify a recent event that scored near the heavenly end of the scale. That's very possible. One friend I tried this on said that he couldn't think of a single event in the recent or distant past that would get a mark above a 5. It wasn't that he particularly disliked individual members of his family; it was when they got together that the fur started to fly and those individual connections got severed.

Part II

Take one of your family get-togethers that you ranked more at the heavenly end of the scale than the hellish end. If, like my friend, it's hard to find one, choose the highest scoring one, even if it's a 5. However, it is likely that for most of you, there will be the occasional good times with your family.

Here are some questions to think about:

- What made it enjoyable?
- How well did your family members get on with each other?
- Was there any friction at all?
- What caused it?
- Did any of it get resolved?
- How did you feel during the get-together?
- How did you feel afterwards?

Now, take a recent event that scores on the hellish end of the scale:

- What made it hellish?
- How well did your family members get on with each other, or not?
- How would you describe the friction?
- What caused it?
- Did any of it get resolved?
- How did you feel during the get-together?
- How did you feel afterwards?

What was the biggest difference between the two events? Were there any particular combinations of 'players' who were especially compatible or especially volatile?

I know in my family when I meet up with some of my siblings it's like settling into an old friendship whenever we're together, whereas with others we're uneasy and uncomfortable and scrounge around for things to talk about.

It may be that in your family, you don't even scrounge around, you head straight for the squabble: someone I only met recently told me that every time he and his two cousins get together they have the same argument they've had for the past 20 years and they no longer even bother with any of the polite niceties of 'Hello, how are you?'

Whatever you and your family do when you're in the hellish end of the spectrum, you've begun your journey and from now on I'll be giving you a variety of things to be aware of and things to try in order to get a little more heaven in your family life.

At the same time, I want to stress that not every family situation is resolvable. Much as you may want to have more enjoyable family get-togethers and are willing to give the suggestions in this book a 'go', the reality is that there are some exceptionally unhealthy families out there and the healthy option may be to remove yourself from that kind of environment. That in itself isn't easy, and I will discuss this later in the book.

However, I wouldn't want you to leap to that option before you read my other ideas. You'll know just what's possible, and through this book you may discover that more is possible than you thought.

Feelings alert

You may have noticed that I keep asking you how you feel about things. I'll continue to do so throughout the book, because feelings inform behaviour.

You will know that there are certain family members whose behaviour hurts, frustrates, enrages or exasperates you, just as there may be those with whom you feel comforted, nurtured, understood and appreciated, or who are just plain fun.

When you're in the midst of all those negative and churned-up feelings, it can feel impossible to see how to change anything for the better. I'll be looking to help you change your behaviour without necessarily changing your feelings first. Look on that as a bonus. If you have to wait to alter what you do till you feel better about some of your family members, you could wait an awfully long time – like forever.

As you read through *Family Heaven, Family Hell* and do the exercises (or even just *think* about doing them), you will have feelings stirred up – one of my guarantees. I know by now you will have already had a few bouncing around inside you. You may also notice that feelings will create thoughts and thoughts will create feelings.

When I was younger and felt jealous of my older sister (which I have fortunately outgrown), my thoughts focused on how much more my parents loved her than they loved me. I had whole Russian novels careening around my head to prove my feelings were right. When it came to my sister, my feelings fed my thoughts and my thoughts fed my feelings in an endless loop of misery. Just as I was able to stay in the stew of my feelings and thoughts, so you may be more tempted to poke around at your feelings than you will be to try out some of the exercises.

Although it's valuable to track your feelings and thoughts (clearly I'm recommending that), this book's aim is to help you survive the family get-together and that will be primarily focusing on what you do. I'll be reminding you about this more than once, because I know from what happens to me that feelings take me by surprise, overwhelm me and then I'm very tempted to act on them, which is not always wise. It does help to remember that a feeling is simply that – a feeling.

Things to be aware of:

Be aware of your family 'cocktail' and if any mixes are more volatile than others.

Be aware of what happens on the hell to heaven scale of your family's behaviour.

Be aware of what makes the difference between a heavenly get-together and a hellish one.

Be aware of some of the expectations you have when with family members.

Be aware of who gets on well with whom and who doesn't.

Be aware of some of the ways you'd like your family members to change which would make get-togethers more bearable.

Be aware of any feelings that get stirred up as you read.

Things you can try:

Nothing to try just yet. Raising your awareness of what happens and how you feel is the perfect first step.

2

Fantasyland vs the Land of Constant Torment

The extremes

Most of the people I've spoken to, and certainly a lot of my own experience, suggest that those of us who don't have the happiest of family gatherings tend to operate out of two extremes when dealing with them: wishful thinking and disheartened hopelessness.

One extreme

Like poor Charlie Brown in *Snoopy* who gets tricked by Lucy every single time, there are many of you who head to your family get-togethers with a conscious or unconscious fantasy that this time it will all be perfect. Everyone will get on; there won't be any tensions, arguments, simmering resentments, jealousies, etc.

Poor Charlie Brown who always falls on his bottom after getting conned once again; poor you who replays all your old patterns while still bewildered that it hasn't changed one little bit.

In Fantasyland, perfection is the height that's aimed for, where people are understanding and kind, empathetic and supportive. Your fantasies get built up each time, and dashed to bits yet again.

Don't you feel sorry for Charlie Brown? Don't you kind of cringe when you see him 'negotiate' with Lucy that this time she really, really, really isn't going to pull the ball away. Promise, promise, you really mean it? You want to say, 'No, Charlie Brown, don't believe her! She's going to do it to you again.' Then you see him fall for her promises and you know the inevitable outcome. Poor Charlie Brown.

We do the same things to ourselves. We talk ourselves into going along to another wedding/christening/naming day/ Sunday lunch, and we work very hard at convincing ourselves that it's going to be OK this time. It's like we try to negotiate with ourselves, 'This time it will be all right, won't it? I'm sure it can't be worse than last time, can it? My son couldn't possibly pull the same stunt as he did before, could he?'

Just the fact that we have those kind of conversations with ourselves shows that we know it's not going to be all right, we know it's going to play itself out the way it always has. Yet, we listen to the siren song of 'You never know, this time it might all be different. I should give people the benefit of the doubt. If I had behaved the way he did, I'd be feeling pretty ashamed, so maybe he'll have seen the light so the next time we get together he won't say those hurtful things.'

Fantasies are seductive, because while we're having them (I certainly know this has been the case with me), we might feel better for a while. All the while we're imagining this enchanting family do, where it's all lovely and loving, we don't have to face up to the truth of what's going on in our families. We get 'duped' by ourselves into believing that somehow, someway, it's going to fix itself.

Case study: Steven's story continued

'How is it that I don't learn? I know what my parents are like. I know that they drink and then they argue. And yet, every time we go out, I think, "This time they'll behave themselves. This time they'll take it easy on the booze and not embarrass themselves and the rest of us." It happens every time, too – sometimes it's really bad, sometimes they just bicker, but they always drink too much. I can't believe that every time I still think it might be different. I know I'm doing it. I know I'm thinking the impossible and yet I can't help it.

'I went to the groom's dinner totally convinced they'd act nice, slow down on the alcohol and the evening would go smoothly. That's why I felt relaxed – I talked myself into believing it was going to be different because it was such a special time.

'I just don't learn. Why would it be any different? Yet, I can't help it. I just can't seem to stop thinking they're going to wake up or something.'

Steven is just like Charlie Brown; he knows what's going to happen, and yet his fantasy of how it could be convinces him that this time his parents will completely change who they are and how they behave in order to fit his fantasy.

And then the other extreme

For many others of you, it's the other extreme: the Land of Constant Torment is more like it. It was my husband, Fred, who came up with that description: he says that when he was younger just thinking about getting together with some members of his family was like being in a state of constant anguish. He tormented himself with reminders of how awful it all was, then he'd feel bad, then he'd remind himself how awful it was, then he'd feel worse. You get the picture.

If this sounds familiar to you, you know you don't live in a Fantasyland; you dread the family get-together, you know exactly what's going to happen. You may not get duped like Charlie Brown but there is a certain inevitability in trying to kick the football anyway and landing on your bum as your metaphorical family-Lucy yanks it away . . . again.

This is equally difficult to deal with because the build-up to getting together is filled with hamster-wheel thoughts about how awful it's going to be, what you're going to say, what they're going to say, what's going to happen.

As soon as the invitation is issued or you set the date, a cloud of gloom is in the back of your mind. You go over the last time you were together, you dissect every conversation, facial expression and hidden meaning. Your heart sinks as you imagine just how awful it's going to be, yet you don't see any way of getting out of it. Then you go along, and you're right – it all plays out just as you expected.

Duty, obligation, guilt all grow in the Land of Constant Torment. It becomes very difficult – even impossible – to see that there's another way to behave or to see that there might be some other action to take.

Much of the conflict and dread, in Fantasyland *and* in the Land of Constant Torment is in trying to reconcile how you want it to be with how it really is.

The Blah Zone

Clearly not everyone experiences their families at these two ends of the spectrum, even those of you who don't have the greatest family events. You're the ones I think of as existing in a kind of neutral Blah Zone: you don't have massive expectations; you don't have huge dreads. You just don't necessarily feel much of anything – you'll go through the motions, wait till it's all over and get back to your normal life.

Even if you're one of the Blah Zonees, you may find this chapter useful anyway, because, undoubtedly, there might very well be members of your family who do function at the emotional extremes and understanding what may be going on for them might be useful in knowing how to deal with them.

I want to go a bit deeper into what happens in these two lands that exist in our heads and feelings.

Fantasyland

You know, Fantasyland isn't just about the great expectations I talked about in Chapter One: how it will all be different and you'll get the love and understanding you yearn for. It isn't only fewer fights, more reasonable discussions and the sweeping away of all those eggshells you walk on. No, Fantasyland has another, more complex element to it: that those family members who have given you a hard time over the years, or made the family get-together difficult and upsetting, will see the error of their ways and admit all the injustices they've done to you and others.

You want apologies, mea culpas and even grovelling. One person I spoke with said it wasn't even enough to get an apology: 'I fantasise about my brother begging for my forgiveness. I imagine him crying and admitting his guilt and shame for having done me wrong.' It's as though the years of accumulated hurts and slights would be wiped away if only they confessed their own terrible behaviour towards you.

This, of course, means that if you don't even get a whiff of an apology or awareness that they might be at fault about anything at all, then your disappointment will be all the greater and, in many cases, the fantasies simply get more bloated: well, *next* time it may turn out better; *next* time they'll be able to see how upset I am and *then* they'll make it all right.

Fantasyland is full of traps like this that will keep you stuck in a revolving door of desire and disappointment.

The Land of Constant Torment

Equally, in the Land of Constant Torment things aren't so straightforward either.

It's not just your anticipation that it's all going to be dreadful; your anxiety that you're going to have the same fights, the same annoyances and the same awful misunderstandings. Oh, no, no, no. In the Land of Constant Torment what happens is that you begin to look for proof that you're right and that it is truly awful. You hear things that perhaps have been said in innocence as sinister and mean. You are ready to pounce on things people say that confirm your worst thoughts and show that you knew it was all going to happen that way just as you had predicted. Your negative thoughts shade much of what happens and it's very hard to see anything other than the very thing you had been anticipating.

Here, too, you are stuck in a revolving door of anxiety and dismay.

Dreams and dread

I suspect that most of you operate with a combination of the two extremes: dread of what might happen and dreams that it will magically change and be better.

It's this see-sawing up and down that can also compound the anxiety beforehand and the disappointment after a family gathering. Our ideal family image or demonised image will make it difficult, if nigh on impossible, to see reality for what it is and therefore see options for change.

This see-sawing can keep us locked in ways of acting that reinforce our beliefs about our most difficult family members. It means that we generally aren't very open to trying a different way. I believe that when we are on this see-saw it's not just that we aren't open to doing things differently, we can't even see that different ways exist – it's not in our vocabulary.

Whichever one it is for you – dreams or dread or a combination of both – keeping it in either stops you from acting differently, from trying new things and from having a realistic viewpoint of what goes on in your family.

The superhero castles in the air

The other fantasy that's equally strong with a lot of (if not most) people is that next time you'll do something really different:

you'll stand up to your mother; you won't let your sister get her own way, you'll confront your abusive uncle.

These fantasies are equally ineffectual. These fantasies cast you in a heroic mould rather than a realistic one. It's unlikely that the behaviour that's required to do these heroic actions is going to be possible. The leap will be too great.

What happens is that you have these fantasies about finally being able to break your bonds and change the patterns of a lifetime – this time you'll have the courage to say all the things you've kept in your head. The only problem is that the behaviour that you display in these daydreams is so far out of character from your normal behaviour that it's highly unlikely you'll ever be able to do it.

Now, having said that, sometimes people have been known to have those explosive moments where everything is so pent up and so volcanic that it finally all bursts out. That, of course, doesn't change anything either as those of you who have let rip will attest. Indeed, it usually makes the situation worse. Of course, I'm not saying the occasional volcanic eruption won't sometimes have the impact you'd hoped – anything is possible. However, as a technique for changing the family dynamics, it rates pretty low on my recommended tactics. You don't have to wreck everything in order to create change; you don't have to have a scorched earth policy to help people see you differently.

What you do need to do is to have behavioural change which fits with your personality and your capacity to communicate differently, rather than become Superman or Wonder Woman.

You are highly unlikely to be able to change your own behaviour which you've been doing your whole life in one fell swoop. If you could, these magical thoughts wouldn't be cramming your brain; you'd be out there doing them. Trying to do something that's outside your communication capability will make you feel a failure and make it more difficult to have a go at something new. If a technique or new tool squares with what you know you can do, then you'll be more likely to use it. Something I suggest might seem like a terrific idea, but if you know you're going to fluff it before you even try, it's a confidence sapper instead of a confidence booster.

In the meantime, it's these unrealistic fantasies that also undermine your confidence, because the more you fantasise about confronting the bully in your family or initiating the heart-to-heart you've always longed for, the less likely you'll actually do it. You may then have the conversations with yourself where you give yourself a severe dressing down for being a coward and not doing what you promised yourself you would do . . . this time.

Case study: Anna's story continued

'I really do feel like a puppet when I'm with my brothers, but the only one pulling the strings is me. I can't seem to help it. I love my mother, but I avoid spending too much time with her now because inevitably one of my brothers will be round there and I know I'll end up first disagreeing with them – especially my older brother – and then giving in and usually crying once I get back to my flat.

'After the funeral, I thought, "That's it. Never again. Next time I'm going to tell them exactly how I feel." Just thinking that felt really good. I began to imagine the conversation. Except it wasn't really a conversation I was imagining – I was picturing me standing in front of him and telling him every awful thing he's ever done. How he's a bully and how he's always trying to control everyone in the family. How things always have to be the way he wants them and he doesn't ever consider any one else's feelings.

'This wasn't the first time I thought about telling him how I felt. Ever since I was a teenager and he used to make my life hell, I thought about screaming at him as loud as I could.

'It never happens though, and it didn't the next time I saw

> him. I smiled, I gave in when he told me what to do. Inside I was seething, and I had my monologue all prepared, but I couldn't do it. Then I felt like a complete idiot and, like always, I gave myself a hard time for being such a wimp and a coward.'

Anna's normal. She's not a wimp or a coward; she simply lives too much in her head imagining a brand new Anna. A brand new Anna isn't what's needed here, but it's often much easier to stay in this hamster-wheel loop than it is to make small changes that might actually get you somewhere.

What I mean is that for many of you it's familiar to imagine becoming a superhero and doing the confronting thing than not doing it and then giving yourself a hard time because you didn't. That's as pernicious a pattern as the ones that you're playing out with your family already.

No wonder it can all feel really stuck.

Not only that, these fantasies are usually inappropriate anyway. You may picture having a righteous rant at your daughter for her thoughtless behaviour, but would that really be suitable? You may feel better about thinking it, but in most cases your fantasies aren't suitable and won't make a difference anyway.

The combination of imagining 'they'll' magically change and you'll transform yourself into the kind of character that exists pretty much only in books and movies is common and, at the same time, unrealistic.

Doesn't your heart just soar when the meek mouse stands their ground and says the perfect, grand and amazingly articulate words such that they cause all around them have their blinkers ripped off and they are humbled in the face of the TRUTH? Most of us (certainly I do) revel when the hero triumphs and the villains get their comeuppance, even more so when the movie/book isn't some implausible adventure story, but more like real life. Then we really imagine it could be us –

we could be in the scenario where the weak become strong, the oppressed break their chains, the verbal knockout punch floors the abuser.

Fat chance.

What has to happen, which is much more realistic, is that you need to identify things you can and know you will do, rather than stay stuck in the fantasies of what you know deep down you never will.

That's why nothing I suggest you do in this book will be about fundamentally changing who you are. I'm not going to lecture you on what you ought to do or how you ought to do it, you're doing that well enough already without me adding my voice to the chatter in your head. I strongly believe this whole process of having better relationships with your family needs to be gentle, gradual and supportive, not setting you impossible targets that will prove disheartening and disabling.

Right now, there's more awareness-raising work to do.

Wishful thinking

Let's look some more at what happens to you in the run-up to some of your family gatherings. In the last chapter, I asked you to take a look at some of your 'great expectations'; now, I want you to get even more specific.

You can use the examples from the hell to heaven scale on page 26 or recall some other recent events. If you can remember, I'd like you to list what you wished was going to be different or what you dreaded most. For instance, I was talking to Robert, a friend of mine, about this. He has one of the richest fantasy lives I know (and I thought I was bad); he told me that before he went to his last family get-together, which was a house-warming party for his in-laws, his wish list went on for about 100 pages. OK, maybe not quite so bad, but here's an example of his before-the-event wishful thinking:

- I wish my wife would stop telling me what to do
- I wish I wouldn't give in so easily when my wife tells me what to do
- I wish my father-in-law would show my kids some affection
- I wish my brother-in-law would congratulate me on my promotion
- I wish my mother-in-law would stop trying so hard to please me

See what I mean? He was so busy making his wish list that, as he put it, 'I didn't really enjoy myself at all because I was so busy waiting for my wishes to come true that I didn't pay attention to what was happening. I only noticed what wasn't happening.'

If you can remember what you wished for (and I bet you will since these most likely won't be brand new wishes, they'll be repeats of age-old ones), you can make your own wish list:

Exercise one

My wish list

Before one of my recent family events I wished:

____

____

____

____

____

Were you disappointed? If so, how disappointed? Extremely, mildly, somewhere in the middle? Or were you more resigned than disappointed? What other feelings did you experience? I know this is a foolish question, but did any of your wishes come true?

If wishes were horses . . .

. . . beggars would ride.

That was a favourite aphorism of my stepmother, who used to say it whenever one of us kids used to wish for something. It was her way of saying, 'highly unlikely'.

It didn't really work – at least it didn't work with me, I don't know about the rest of my siblings. All I know is that no matter what she said, I'd keep on wishing.

So, I'm going to suggest that it's highly unlikely any of your wishes are going to come true, but I doubt that's going to stop you wishing them anyway. That's how we keep the patterns going: we wish for something, it doesn't happen and then we keep right on wishing.

Like Robert, though, all those wishes can keep us from actually being present with our families because our attention is focused on what isn't changing, what they haven't done and how bad you might feel about it.

The same is true for those of you who enter the Land of Constant Torment.

Exercise two

Now let's do the opposite. If you have experiences of being in the Land of Constant Torment, now is the time to list them.

These torments usually take the form of loads of negative thoughts about what happened last time and what's likely to happen this time. That hamster wheel goes round and round reminding you of the embarrassing, unpleasant, uncomfortable and gut-wrenching things some members of your family did. What torments you about your family?

Before a recent family gathering I found myself thinking:

____

____

____

____

____

____

Were you right? Did it all pan out the way you expected it to? What were your feelings before, during and after?

As in the previous exercise, it often happens that we get so focused on noticing the dreadful things others are doing that we can't see much beyond that.

The eye of the storm

Have you ever been in a hurricane? If you haven't experienced one in real life, have you ever watched any TV programmes about them? In the simplest terms, a hurricane is a swirling mass of storm which hurtles itself from the sea and blows onto land, devastating (in the worst cases) all before it. Right in the middle is the eye of the storm, an eerily calm bit where everything is silent and still before it all starts up again.

Not all bad or uncomfortable family get-togethers are like hurricanes, but sometimes it can feel as though you are in the midst of something like a force of nature which you can't control. You can't control a hurricane but there will be things you can do to feel more in charge of what happens around you.

To begin, I'm asking you to enter the eye of the storm, the calm and still time where there might be enough silence for you to see what is good about your family, what you do like about certain members of your clan, what they do do that you enjoy and take delight in. The maelstrom may still be poised to descend any minute, but for now, let's take some quiet time to assess what might be positive in your family.

In the last chapter, I asked you to take a family event that was at the heavenly end of the scale and unpick it a little. Now, I'd like you to look at some of the individual members of your family – those you get on with and those you don't – and do a bit of unpicking here as well.

Exercise three

Since we're dealing with extremes, let's carry on the same theme. Make a list of those with whom you get on best and those with whom you get on least well.

Name	What I like about them

It's wonderful being with people you get on with and whose company you enjoy. There are times when I'm with my mother and older sister where we spend most of our time laughing, because in many instances we all seem to have the same outlook on life and laugh at the same absurdities. My youngest sister has a wicked, slightly sardonic way of phrasing things (a really quick wit) and it's great fun getting her 'take' on life. I don't see her as much as I'd like, but being with her is always a delight.

Much harder at the other extreme.

Name	What they do that gets up my nose

Just thinking about certain people in my family, I can get all worked up. Things that I would tolerate in someone I really like, I find incredibly annoying in people I don't. I know I'm not alone in that – I bet the same is true for you as well. Think about it. Take one example of something someone does that you don't like, say, for instance, sitting in front of the TV when you come in and not saying hello. How rude! It's much easier to feel resentful and stomp off into the kitchen and make a comment about it when it's to do with someone you don't like.

Imagine the same scenario with someone you do like. You walk in, they're sat in front of the telly not saying anything, and most likely you won't stomp into the kitchen, you'll cuff them on the back of the head or tease them or say something mock-mean to get their attention. In other words, you won't hold it against them, will you? Unlikely. They're your buddy – you could plop next to them on the sofa and tickle them or even turn off the telly and it will feel easy to do. Even imagining doing the same thing with people you don't feel so good about may seem impossible.

It's when we don't like someone or don't get on with them that we go back to doing that proof-finding thing I mentioned earlier in the chapter – how you'll pounce on their behaviour to prove you were right all along.

Interesting this, and I'll be coming back to this theme later. Right now, I have something else with which to challenge you.

Exercise four

I'd like you to see if you can identify any positive and likeable qualities in the members of your family you get on with least well. For some of you this may be very tricky; I know that I resist this bit and I'm a tad grudging about acknowledging anything positive in those I get on with badly. Don't despair, there's a long way to go in this book and you can go back to resenting them in a few minutes.

For the moment, try to get beyond what they do that gets up your nose to see if there's anything about them you could say, 'Actually, she does make an effort when we're all together,' or 'He does seem to entertain Mother and that's saying a lot,' or 'I'm impressed with how well they bring up their kids.'

Case study: Christine's story continued

'There isn't anything in my brother-in-law I like, I can tell you that flat-out.'

I had asked Christine to try this exercise and as you can see at first she found it impossible. We persevered and I asked her what she thought her sister saw in him. Her first reaction was, 'I haven't a clue.'

Then she thought about it some more, and this is what she had to say:

'I find this very hard. Geoff has disrupted our cosy family and everything feels a mess so I resent having to find something nice to say about him, but here goes. My sister, Lisa, obviously loves him.

'He's a good provider, I will say that. He's the first boyfriend she's ever had with a proper job who isn't always asking her for money. So I guess he's responsible.

'He has good manners: opening doors, pulling chairs out, things like that.

'He says flattering things about us, but I think that's just to get on our good sides.'

Notice that little 'but' at the end there?

When I'm searching high and low to find something complimentary about people I don't get on with, I'm guilty of adding just such a rider, so it doesn't sound as though I'm giving in completely and starting to like the person more than I dislike them. I seem to want to hold on to my dislikes. Writing this book has brought me right up against my own unhelpful patterns, as I suspect (and hope) it will with yours as well.

So here it goes:

People I don't like all that much	**Some of their good qualities**

How was that to do? Did you find yourself slipping in any of those little addenda I'm guilty of tacking on in order to take the sting out of saying something positive?

In some cases it really is black and white – 'they' really are beyond the pale. However, when we take apart the family get-together and the 'players' in your own personal drama, most people will have something positive about them that usually gets smothered in all the things you don't like.

Back into the storm

Having taken a few quiet (did *I* say quiet?) minutes to look at some of the more positive aspects of individuals in your family, we're back to more of the nitty-gritty of what happens at your family get-togethers.

I want to take a different perspective on dreads and dreams. I call this a Fantasy Mind Map.

Have you ever done a mind map? Some people find them very useful to examine issues and situations from a slightly different angle. A mind map starts with a circle in the middle of a page with satellite circles coming out from it with their own little satellite circles or lines. You put a word or phrase in the middle one and see what words or phrases pop into your head. It's a little bit like free association, where one word will lead you to another and another. By doing this, sometimes interesting and useful patterns emerge which may clarify some things for you.

Here's an example of what I mean to give you a better picture of what to do, if you decide to give it a try. I'm using my friend Robert as a guinea pig here since he was so willing to talk to me about his wish list.

After Robert drew his map he said, 'Wait a minute! This is all about me being noticed.' He hadn't seen before that what was fuelling some of his fantasies was that he wanted his family to pay attention to him and acknowledge him both for what he'd accomplished and for who he was. He realised that his wishes weren't just based on how he wanted 'them' to behave, but on how he wanted to feel when he was with them.

Robert's Fantasy Mind Map

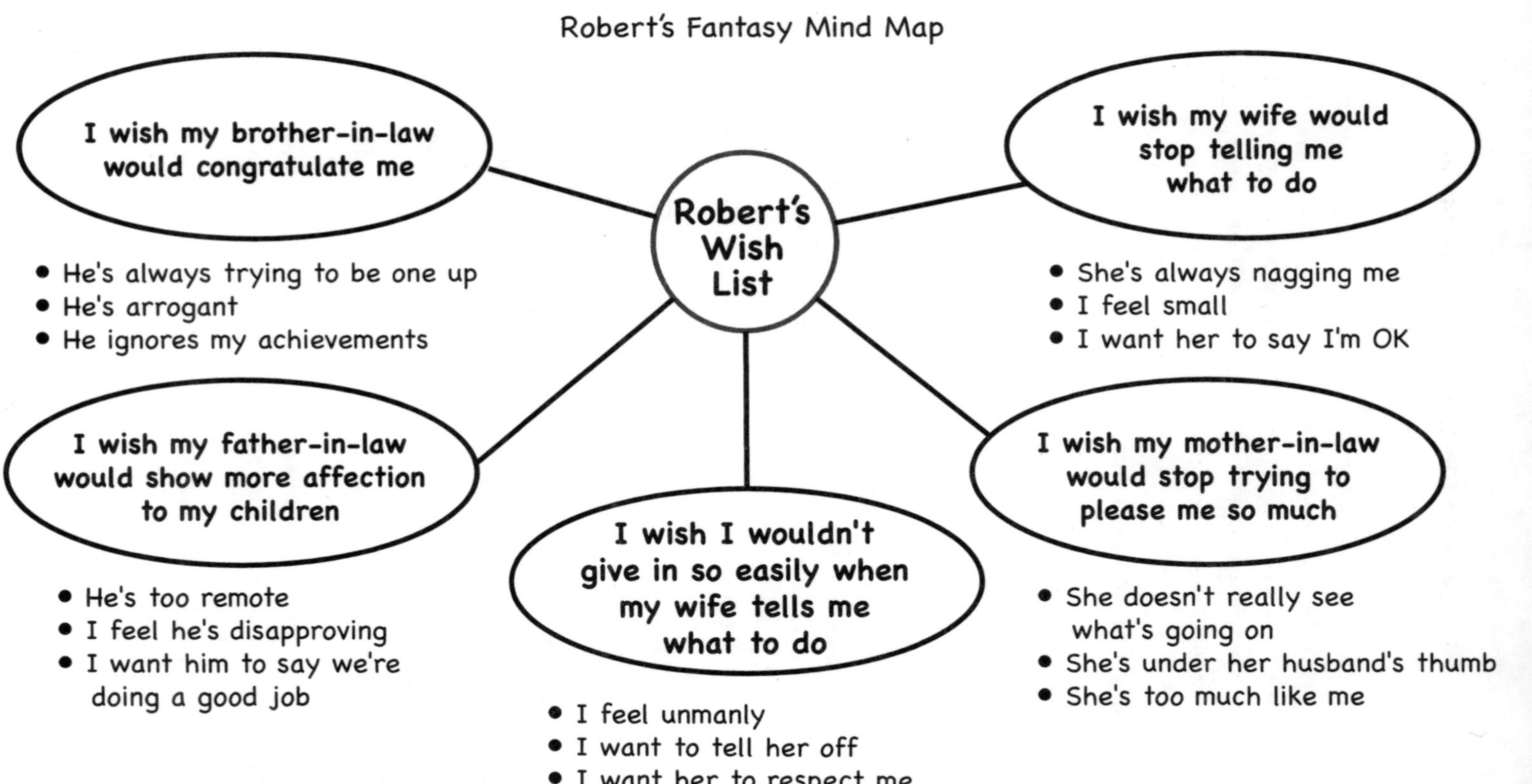

In order to feel better and enjoy his get-togethers more, Robert fantasised about them changing their behaviour, which in turn would give him what he needed. He hadn't seen it that way before at all; before it was all about what they weren't doing that made some of his get-togethers so uncomfortable for him. Just doing the Fantasy Mind Map helped him see that there was a lot more going on than just their behaviour.

Exercise five

Now it's your turn

You can put anything in the centre of your Fantasy Mind Map: one single wish, one single dread, or the whole kit and caboodle as Robert did, where his satellite circles were the specific fantasies. The important thing is to write down whatever pops into your head whether it makes sense or not. Just write your thoughts or associations down as quickly as possible without editing anything. This is for you after all, no one is going to be 'grading' you on how well you do your Fantasy Mind Map.

Once you finish filling it all in, take a closer look and see if you can identify any themes or consistent feelings and thoughts as Robert did. You might want to circle those in a different colour pen so they stand out.

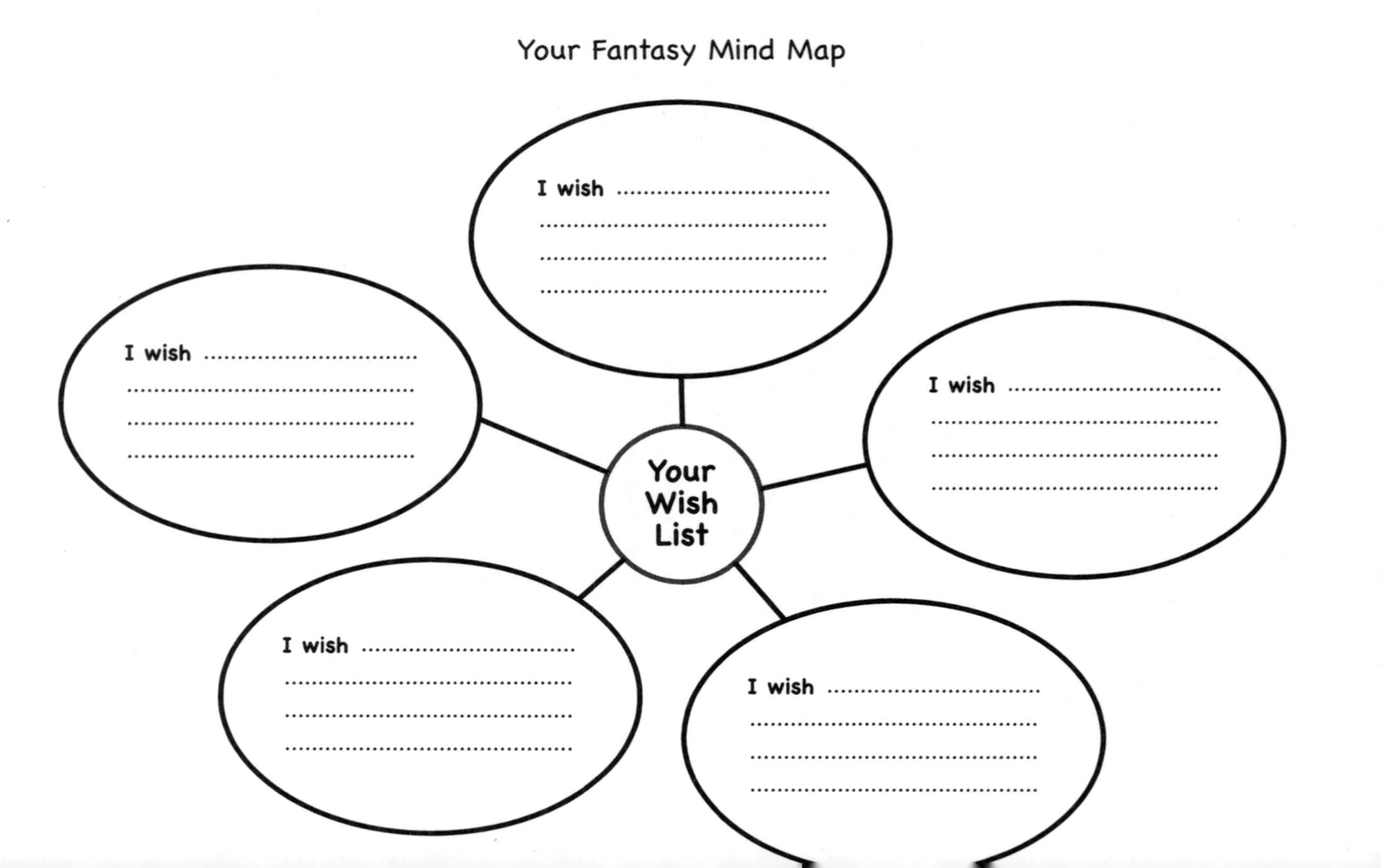
Your Fantasy Mind Map
I wish
Your Wish List
I wish
I wish
I wish
I wish

Turning the map upside down

Now it's time for a redraw.

There are many schools of thought and psychology that say you can 'reprogramme' or even trick your brain into thinking in another way. I think of it more as easing you into looking at things slightly differently so that from there you can see what behavioural changes might be possible.

In these early chapters my aim is to kick-start you thinking in different ways and to give you greater insight into what happens when you are with your family. Whether that's tricking your brain or reprogramming, it doesn't really matter. The outcome is to be open to new ideas so that from there you can initiate new ways of behaving which might make your next family event a far happier one.

So here's a technique to turn your Fantasy Mind Map on its head. This is not about the first thing that pops into your mind, but about drawing a different conclusion to the same wish.

In the first map, Robert could only see his wishes in light of how he felt and what he wasn't receiving. His fantasies could never be fulfilled because they were based on people changing their behaviour to make his feeling all right. When I asked Robert to redraw his map this is what I asked him to do: 'Write down your wishes as before, but this time instead of those stream of consciousness thoughts branching out from every wish, see if you can find a positive association for each one.'

Here's what his redrawn map looks like:

Robert's redrawn map

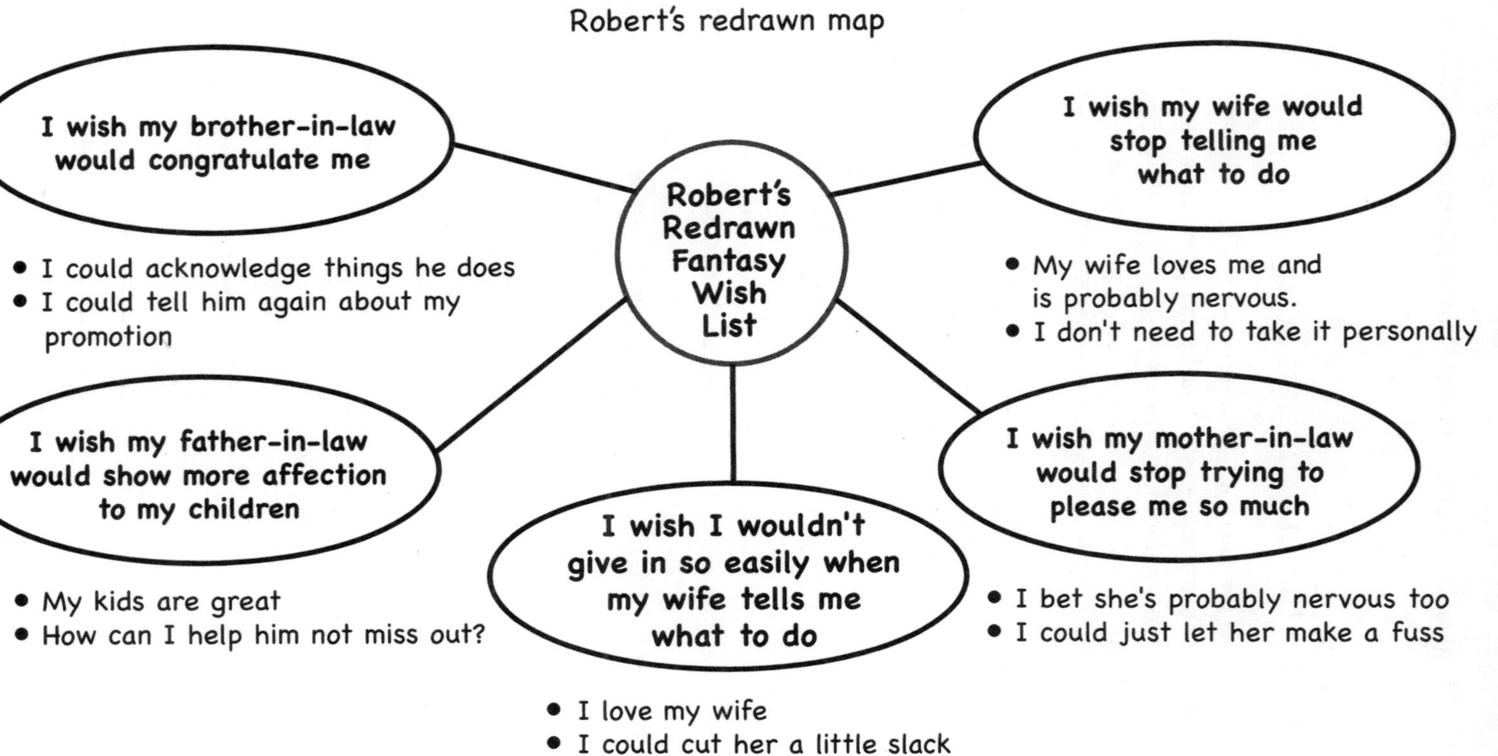

Exercise six

Your turn

Using the same wishes as before, fill in your Fantasy Mind Map to arrive at positive courses of action or to achieve more positive thoughts and feelings. You don't have to do anything just yet – that will come later when I've introduced you to some new techniques to practise.

Your new Fantasy Mind Map

Grab a sheet of blank paper and redraw your map. If you've been able to redraw your map, can you identify how you feel about it (there I go again, asking you how you feel)? Does it feel odd? Uncomfortable? In the Blah Zone?

If you have the desire, you can now do the same exercises, but putting your torments/dreads in the centre circle and first do your word association and then redraw your map to include some positive outcomes or possible actions.

My aim here is to get you to see that there are other options in nearly every situation. Whether you do them or not is another matter, but right now it's good to see that you have the option of looking at your fantasies as wishes that will never be fulfilled or as wishes that could have a completely different outcome. As dreads that you will always encounter or as dreads that could be stopped in their tracks and turned around.

Things to be aware of:

Be aware of the fantasies you have before your next family get-together.

Be aware of any torments you are expecting to happen at your next family get-together.

Be aware if you're expecting a miracle to happen and for the scales to fall off someone's eyes and for them to suddenly treat you differently.

Be aware if you are seeking proof that your expectations of other people's bad behaviour is true.

Be aware if you're resistant to finding anything positive about people you don't get on with that well.

Things you could try:

Try to step back and see if you can find positive qualities in the family members you get on with least well.

Try drawing a number of Fantasy/Dread Mind Maps and redrawing them with positive outcomes.

Identify how you feel when drawing a turned-on-its-head map.

3

Home and Away

Fred and Jo Ellen's story

Once upon a time, in the early years of my marriage, my husband Fred and I used to get together with his parents on an occasional basis. They lived about an hour away in New Jersey (we were in New York City then) and just about the time we hit the New Jersey Turnpike (a nightmare in itself), the family get-together jitters would set in.

Fred dreaded the visits (both parents were alcoholics) and I had to steel myself for a most uncomfortable afternoon. The get-togethers were always tense. His parents were desperate to see us, but were so involved in their own entrenched warfare that they sniped at each other through us.

His father clearly looked forward to our coming but as soon as we entered the house, he would disappear out back. His mother would hang out in the kitchen showing us stuff she had either acquired or unearthed from mouldy boxes stashed in the attic or basement: fading photographs, broken bits of china, old dolls. Fred's bewildered, unpleasant and equally alcoholic grandfather stayed in his room upstairs (Fred's mother referred to him as 'the old goat'), an invisible but audible presence. Not invisible, but equally audible, was the chicken that hung out in the living room.

There would always be mountains of food (most of it not very good) with an expectation that we would eat a goodly portion of it.

We did the minimum: ate what was humanly manageable, stayed to the minute of acceptability and made as seemly a dash to the car as we could without appearing to want to get the hell out of there. The car was always filled with the bits of things his mother had found, furniture that needed repairing and a serious number of containers of inedible food.

About 20 minutes into the drive back, I'd have to pull over to the side of the road so Fred could vomit. That would signal the onset of a killer migraine which would last at least a couple of days.

The emotional impact of those get-togethers was profound and the disconnected relationships between Fred and his parents was disturbing. Those visits summed up, in an extreme way, what happens in families all the time.

Great distances exist that we try to bridge because most of us want a family, and we will tolerate these distances in trying to create the closeness we desire.

After a few years of this, I finally put my foot down and said I wasn't going any more. I couldn't bear seeing him suffer and I found the get-togethers intolerable.

Fred, too, eventually stopped going and, finally, quietly and with no temperamental fanfare, stopped seeing them altogether, though he continued the relationship by phone, which was far easier for him to manage.

In reminding myself of this part of our history, I have seen this whole aspect of our lives in a new context: the context of why family get-togethers can be so unendurable. Indeed, why family get-togethers can be damaging to one's health if the same old patterns are played out time and time again. And unless changed, those patterns usually do play themselves out over and over.

I realise, too, that although our decisions were appropriate at the time, neither of us had the maturity then to see that perhaps there might have been another way to deal with what seemed like an impossible situation. It may very well be that walking away, as we each did in our own way, was the best thing we could have done then and now, if the situation was repeated. However, we each of us lacked the ability to understand that we did have other options: we were blinded by the family patterns we were used to and, therefore, we could only react through those patterns. As I've got 'older and wiser', I realise that many of the options I write about in this book were available to us then; we just couldn't see them.

Reflecting on all of this also gave me insight into the fundamental difference between happy families and unhappy ones and helped me see the key to how to survive the family get-together.

In this chapter, I'll be offering you the start of a good grounding in what happens at a lot of family get-togethers and the first steps you'll need to gain the insight and behaviour change needed in order to turn your family get-togethers from hell to heaven (or a reasonable proximity thereof).

This is the understanding I myself gained when unpicking my and Fred's relationships with his parents, and helped me see the family get-together in a new light. This indeed helped me see the difference between family heaven and family hell.

It's not rocket science, though with some families it can certainly feel like you're facing a mathematical problem you'd have to be an Einstein to solve. That's because logic has nothing to do with it: family get-togethers are filled to bursting with emotions, history, patterns, expectations, yearnings (a word I'll be using frequently), fantasies and resentments.

In the last chapter, I asked you to look at some of your family get-togethers. Now I'd like you to look at the impact a couple of your family members have on you to get the ball rolling.

Exercise one

With your eyes closed, think about someone in your family you really like, get on with and find easy to be with. When you are with them, you don't really have to alter yourself much: you don't have to put on a mask, pretend to be someone you're not or act one way while feeling completely different inside.

What are your feelings when you think about this family member? Do you have that 'warm and fuzzy' feeling? Do you smile when you imagine them chatting with you? Do you feel tender or energised or excited?

You might want to begin writing any feelings and thoughts you have as you do these and other exercises. If you're not much of a writer or don't like expressing yourself that way, you could try drawing your feelings and thoughts. If the idea of drawing makes you cringe, you can speak your feelings aloud in an empty room or to a good friend.

Expressing your feelings is a good way of making them valid. Too often we dismiss how we feel or are embarrassed by our feelings. If you're one of those people, now would be a great time to let your feelings have a bit of breathing space.

What conclusions can you draw from your relationship with this family member?

Exercise two

Now think about the person in your family you get on with least well: you don't find it easy to be with them; you dread seeing them; you feel as though you have to play out a different 'you' in order to get through the get-together.

Again, what are your feelings when you think about this family member? Do you have any physical responses? For instance, when I think of the person with whom I get on least well, my stomach clenches and I kind of sigh like I have the burdens of the world on my shoulders even though I haven't seen this person for years and years.

What conclusions can you draw from your relationship with this family member?

I know that the differences between these two exercises may be extreme. I can think with great warmth about my twin cousins whom I hardly ever see; the last time was a few years ago when they visited the UK. It felt great to be with them and I felt relaxed and easy and fully myself. On the other hand, there are other members of my family, who, when I am with them, everything tenses up; I feel as though I'm 'holding myself together' and I am not at ease until it's over. I breathe a huge sigh of relief and put aside my 'false' self like a dress that has never fitted but is kept in my closet anyway, hoping the next time I wear it, it will somehow magically look better (more on this aspect of family get-togethers later).

Similarly, in the first scenario, my guess is that you are in easy and welcome territory; in the second you are uneasy, tense and in what feels like completely alien territory (no matter how familiar it may seem) where you are not fully yourself.

'Alien territory'. That's a strange term to give a family get-together, but as far as I can see, when a family get-together feels like hell, then that's what you're in.

Alien territory

So let's define 'alien territory' in relation to the family get-together. This is the place where it doesn't look and feel right, no matter how *familiar* it is (because you've been there so many times before). It feels uncomfortable, possibly unsafe, certainly out of balance. We're just not ourselves; we're wary, walking on eggshells. We stop being our true, authentic selves and become someone else who may not even look and sound completely like our true selves (when I was much younger I could, even in my unaware state way back then, hear my normally animated, colourful voice become flat in my determination to give nothing away). The key feature of the family get-together alien territory is that it stays the same, behaviours get stuck and nothing changes.

Indeed, the arguments and bickering that go on in this alien territory are often fuelled by a need to get the other person to understand us better, see the world through our eyes, agree that we're right (and in turn, that they are wrong) and we'll often seemingly fight to the metaphorical death to hold on to our point of view.

The family dynamics are stuck.

So what do I mean by family dynamics? It's a great word, isn't it? It means to move things forward, to be energetic, lively, active, go-getting. The word has been commandeered by the psychology world in relation to families and other relationships to describe what happens between people: what is the energy that exists in relationships? How well or badly do people get on with each other?

For instance, in what's known as healthy family dynamics, things are constantly developing and changing; relationships within the family are active and energetic. In unhealthy dynamics, things are still moving, but they move in a perpetual loop: relationships between people stay stuck in the same ways of behaving as they've always done. Sometimes, unhealthy dynamics are caused by secrets or dishonesty which create their own tensions because they sit under the surface even though no one may actually talk about them.

In Chapter One, for instance, I used the term 'culture clash' to describe some of the difficulties families face. This can come about through differing values and widely contrasting outlooks on life. Sometimes secrets are kept in order not to hurt others in the family or force them to face facts that are completely antithetical to their beliefs.

Case study: Nisar's story

Nisar is 26, and lives in Karachi. He has a large and very extended family, most of whom also live in the capital. When he was an undergraduate, he spent three years in the UK studying to be an engineer at Cambridge University.

'I love my family and my family loves me. Everyone is expected to come to my parents' house every Friday evening for dinner after the working week and for Sunday lunch as well. My mother will have spent the entire week preparing and cooking for these meals. She is a great traditional cook and now that my grandmother is too ill to interfere, she has the kitchen to herself.

'Although my father was always very strict with us, we all have a fun time together now that we children are all grown. My sisters are all married and my brother is engaged and we can be quite boisterous when we're all in the same place at the same time. We enjoy teasing each other and we're all very affectionate, even my dad.

'I could say that we're as near perfect as you could want, but for one thing. I'm gay. I can't come out. Although my family are fairly liberal as far as our culture goes, you just can't be gay. It has to stay a frightening secret.

'When I was studying in England, I went to see *East is East** five times in a row. My father isn't as dictatorial as the father in the film, but I know my mother and father couldn't handle it if I came out. We're Muslim, how could I even think of it! The story was a huge relief to me, but I just haven't been able to face my parents' disgust or disapproval. I can't even begin to think it in terms of the society I live in.

'This makes going to visit them a complete nightmare. I'm teased by everyone in the family about when am I going to meet a nice girl; maybe they'll have to go to a marriage broker to find one; I'm too shy; Auntie so-and-so must know the perfect partner. I couldn't believe my ears when my mother even said that if I wanted to live with someone first before getting married, they'd understand. That's totally forbidden in the Koran, but clearly she's feeling desperate.

'The awful thing about it all is that I have a boyfriend, Kasim, and if he was a girl they'd love him. I'm living a lie

> whenever I am with my family. I live a lie all the time. Kasim and I are "just good friends".
>
> 'I kind of think one of my sisters knows and possibly even my mother might guess, but I can't say anything because I don't want to lose their love.'

(*For those of you who haven't seen *East is East*, it's a film that takes place in 1970s Britain and is the story of a mixed-race family with a British mother and Pakistani father. One of the storylines has to do with the eldest son. He is gay, abandons an arranged marriage and is disowned by his father.)

Nisar's hell isn't old family feuds or stored up resentments or deep hurts. Nonetheless, his family get-togethers aren't free and easy because he knows he can't be honest. He is probably right that he will be cut off from his family or worse, if they find out, but Nisar is in alien territory. He can't be fully himself and in some ways part of his happy family life is a facade he has erected to protect himself. He feels alien all the time, but the one refuge he might have – his family – is also out of bounds.

Alien territory comes in many guises; the consistent feature is that you have to alter who you are and how you behave when you enter it.

There is such a thing as a heavenly family

In happy families, fights still happen: people sulk and slam doors and flounce and rail and blame. The difference between family heaven and family hell is that with happy families all that angst is resolvable because things evolve. Family dynamics don't stay stuck for very long and things develop and change because enough family members are willing to make changes.

Here's an example of a heavenly family I know:

This is a family that loves get-togethers and parties. They spend endless hours planning anniversary parties and surprise birthday parties. They love Christmas, going on family outings with as many of their extended 'gang' that can make it and get excited even if it's a simple Sunday lunch together.

Now this family does have its difficulties. They have squabbles, jealousies, get mad at each other: everything that happens with a hellish family. Not everyone likes each other equally; they gossip and occasionally stir things up just like anyone else.

But over the years that I've known them I've been aware that they are never 'static'. They will always look for a way to resolve difficulties, even if it involves compromise. And more importantly, I have never seen them stop being anything other than their authentic selves when they are with each other; even when one family member doesn't like another one all that much.

As I know some of them separately as well as together, I see that they don't 'change' themselves when they are at their family gatherings; they are who they are. Of course, they may adapt their behaviour slightly to suit the situation, but never to the extent of being inauthentic. They aren't in alien territory because if something feels uncomfortable, they work at it till it sorts itself out.

If they have arguments, they aren't the same arguments they had ten years ago. When someone new enters the family fold, they work to include them as much as possible rather than waiting till they prove themselves first.

They aren't perfect; no family is. They simply don't want to stay stuck, so their behaviour reflects that, even in tough times.

In family hell, old patterns get repeated endlessly and people either don't recognise that change is possible or don't have the skills or the will to do so.

When even your own home is against you

It's bad enough when you go to a family gathering away from home and it feels dreadful. But it's really depressing when the family event is at your own home and instead of feeling welcoming and excited about it, you find yourself preparing to be invaded by the enemy hordes. Your own home can feel unsafe and you have no place to hide. That's the power of family dynamics where you find yourself changing your 'normal' behaviour and you're waiting for the other shoe to drop. Who scattered all those eggshells in your own home!

It's a strange thing that the family influence can be such that you don't even call the shots or set the tone of the family get-together when it's in your home territory: the patterns, history and relationships are such that they 'rule', take over and set the mood, not you.

Most people I've spoken to about this say they much prefer going to someone else's house or to a neutral (is there such a thing?) gathering place than have people they don't really want to 'occupy' their home. At least when you're out you can always leave, which might give you the illusion of being somewhat in control of the situation. At home, you're stuck until others choose to make their exit.

So, unfortunately, your own home can feel like alien territory, and if you're anything like me, you count the minutes till you have your own home back, and you rush around clearing up, plumping cushions, doing things to get the place back to being yours again.

Home territory

When you go to a stressful, difficult family get-together you are going into a different 'world' where the rules of engagement change.

Let's go back to exercise one, where you looked at what it feels like to be with someone from your family who you really like. Your behaviour will most likely reflect what you feel. If you feel relaxed, you'll behave differently than when you feel tense. In a way you could call this home territory, where you feel and behave most like yourself.

Exercise three

Much like the first exercise, remind yourself of your behaviour when you are in home territory.

Of course, your behaviour will change somewhat with each person you relate to. However, overall, how you act with your favourite family members is unlikely to be too different from when you are with your closest friends (indeed, it's even possible some of your family *are* your best friends).

What are some of things you do? How do you welcome someone into your home territory? I know that I always have a big smile, am open-armed with a big hug if appropriate, offer the contents of my cupboards and fridge and can't wait to get settled and cosy up for a good chat. Even if I'm in a bad way and feeling vulnerable or teary, that first greeting will tend to be the same.

If you're someone who likes the visual, can you 'see' what this home territory looks like? Is it a sunny beach, a cosy room in front of a fire, a garden? My home territory, for example, is a very solid house with comfortable furniture, lots of books and people all chatting with each other.

This is always the easy bit – when I feel at home, I just can't wait to be with the people I love, and I love treating them well.

If you take time to observe your own behaviour when in home territory over the next few weeks, you'll be able to see more clearly how you change it when you go into alien territory.

Defining your alien territory

Again, going back to exercise two, when you imagined being with someone from your family who you don't get on with, even without consciously realising it, your behaviour will also reflect how you feel.

It may not be out and out war, but, like me, your voice may

change, your body language might get more restrained (mine does) or just the opposite, more frantic; you certainly won't be cosying up for a nice chat.

Exercise four

If you can remember the last family get-together that didn't go so well, see if you can identify how your 'normal' behaviour changed. What did you do differently?

One of the things I realise I used to do was to get incredibly efficient. I did efficient things like make sure the table was set (even if it wasn't my house) and that things were organised for setting out nibbles or getting the meal ready. I kept myself busy in order to avoid too much talk that might have lead to the inevitable disagreement.

I have a friend whose voice used to go up about two octaves whenever she spent time with her family and she absolutely didn't realise it till we got talking after the one and only time I spent with her family at a birthday party. Sometimes we know exactly what our behaviour is like, but often we fall into behaviour we don't consciously know we're doing. How do you alter yourself when you enter alien territory?

If we add the visual, can you 'see' what this alien territory looks like? Is it a bleak landscape, a jungle, a raging river? When I think of what represents my alien territory, I see a kind of half desert, half mountainous setting with no vegetation and people kind of standing around with vast distances in between and not really looking at each other. On the other hand, Fred says his alien territory is a normal-looking house, but inside the air is crackling with tension so strong it feels as though he could touch it.

On the face of it, it does seem strange to call attending a family get-together going into alien territory, but how else to describe the feeling that you simply don't belong? Or don't belong when you're with certain family members.

Case study: Tim's story

Tim, 38, is a middle-school teacher and has a brother who is three years older. Tim sees his family for the big occasions – Christmas, parents' anniversaries and birthdays – and tries to avoid any others.

'I know it's a joke when you hear people say they must have been switched at birth because they seem so different from their family. Well, I'm sure it must have happened to me, and I wish I could go out and find my real family; ones who won't argue whenever we see each other.

'OK, I really do know it's a joke, but ever since I was a little kid I thought there must be another, better family out there looking for me who would rescue me from this fake family. I felt a complete stranger in my own home and I still do whenever I go to visit my parents or brother.

'I like that you call it alien territory because when I look at my family, they *are* aliens. How could we possibly have the same DNA?

'I'm sceptical that anything you tell me to do is going to make any difference, but I'll give it a go. I can't imagine them changing though.'

You're right, Tim, they aren't going to change. It's you who's going to have to make the effort if anything is going to be different. Yet, this is how most of us wish it would be – that others change to make things easier for ourselves. I'll be going into far more detail on this in Chapter Four.

However, a very important point to make here is that a lot of people feel the way Tim does – joke or no joke – that they really don't belong to the families they have. Many psychotherapists and psychologists remark on this yearning we have that the perfect family exists somewhere and it definitely isn't the one we already have. We often feel so disconnected to our own 'flesh and blood' that we can't quite accept that yes, indeed, we all belong to the same family.

Although there are extremely rare cases of babies being switched at birth, to the vast majority of people across the world, the family you've got is yours, like it or not. The yearning for another, better, family (as Tim puts it) is us trying to convince ourselves that these aliens aren't really our family at all. How could we be part of *that*?!

This 'better' family will love us warts and all; they'll appreciate us and really be able to 'see' us for who we are. This is the miracle family those of us with difficult ones fantasise about, and our get-togethers would be fantastic with this replacement family.

Many adopted children feel this very keenly; if they are unhappy with the family who have adopted them, they are convinced that their 'real' family will be far more understanding, kind and loving.

So what's all this about and why does it impact on the family get-together so thoroughly?

Belonging

There are some misanthropes out there. There are some hermits and recluses who hide themselves away and have little to do with society at just about any level. The rest of us? We want to belong. In some form or another, we want to be part of something. However enraged we are with our families, one of the reasons we hold on to that rage is because we want it to be better and we can't bear it when it isn't. We want to be part of something and our frustration when it doesn't happen the way we want can be huge.

Case study: Morris's story

Morris is 62, a hard-nosed New Yorker working as a civil servant in New York City government. His mother is 85 and his only sister is a year younger than him.

'You talk about becoming inauthentic when you're with family members. I am completely inauthentic when I'm with my mother and sister. I am utterly consumed with thoughts of vengeance, jealousies, resentments and angers.

'When I see them together they seem to have something between them that excludes me. I feel betrayed that they are connecting with each other but not with me – I feel left out of the connection. I want what they seem to be giving each other.

'I can't believe that here I am 62 years old and I'm still whacked by the same impossible emotions I had when I was ten. I don't even know if it's real, what I'm thinking. Maybe they aren't giving each other anything special, but that doesn't seem to stop my murderous thoughts.

'The stupid thing is I keep going back for more. I keep going back in the hopes I'll get that connection. If I haven't got it yet, what are the chances I'm going to get it any time soon?'

Strong emotions, but Morris's story perfectly illustrates the need to belong; that even in the face of feeling left out and excluded he still wants that connection and keeps going back in the hopes of getting it.

You could say that's why many people try to turn their work colleagues into family, or join clubs or make friends their surrogate families. You could say it's one of the key reasons kids join gangs.

Have you noticed the huge proliferation in books and TV programmes encouraging us to discover our roots, create our family tree, find out where we come from, who do you think we are, etc? It seems the more we are dispersed, move around, intermarry, the more we want to find out about our backgrounds. In other words, we want to know where we belong and how we fit in. This may be especially strong when we don't really feel we fit in with the family we're in the middle of.

And because most of us aren't misanthropes or hermits or recluses, we do need families in some form. The trouble comes when the families we've got prove disappointing and we don't feel we belong. Somehow, if we discover that Great-great-uncle Charles threw over the traces, left his family and became a missionary in Africa, it might somehow justify our own dissatisfaction and desire to chuck in our families.

Maybe you've already delved into your family history and found out all sorts of fascinating things, or maybe you've simply thought about doing it. However, I'm far more interested in helping you deal with the here and now, in looking more deeply at the family that's right in front of you.

It's worth taking a look at how you feel in relation to the various members of your family; where you feel a connection and where you feel a separation; where you feel you don't belong.

Exercise five

There's a very good exercise or process that is used in some forms of psychotherapy, family therapy and group therapy. It's called family sculpting and in its simplest form is a three-dimensional way of seeing yourself in relation to the various members of your family.

In family therapy, actual family members are used; in other group settings the different people in the group represent a person's individual family members. For the purposes of this exercise, I'm going to suggest using objects in place of real people so you can carry it out on your own.

Gather together a variety of objects, knick-knacks, decorations. Assign a family member, including yourself, to each object. The objects in and of themselves don't have to have any special meaning, unless you choose to assign a person to an object that seems to bring them to life. For instance, if you have a comforting relationship with your mother, you might choose a teapot as her object. Conversely, if you have a fiery relationship with her, you might choose a book of matches.

Again, if you would rather draw or write, rather than use specific objects, that will be just as effective.

Make some space on the floor or on a table. Place the object that represents you in the middle. Then place the remaining 'family members' in relation to you. Space them out in terms of how close or remote you feel your relationship is with each individual.

Stand back from it all and get an overview. Change anything that doesn't feel quite right.

What does it feel like seeing your family represented in this way? With whom do you feel closest? And with whom most alienated? Like Morris, are there any family alliances that give you a sense of being excluded or disconnected?

Simple as this version of family sculpting is, I find even in this form it can bring up some very strong emotions.

When I look at my own sculpture, I notice that I've placed just a few of my family near me and the rest could be in someone else's sculpture, they are so emotionally remote from me. On the other hand, I come from a huge extended family on my mother's side and though I don't know them all and hardly ever see any of them, I do have a sense of being part of this vast network of people dotted around the US.

Looking at your family from this perspective, can you identify any additional ways you change your behaviour when you are with people who aren't so close to you in your sculpture? Any other ways you find yourself being less authentic or wearing a mask?

The exercises in this chapter have been designed to raise your awareness of some of the dynamics that happen when you get together with members of your family. They set the scene for the rest of the book where I will be offering you suggestions of things you might do differently.

What is important is that at this point in your journey, the one thing you can't change yet is how you feel. Whether you feel disconnected, alienated, uncomfortable, frustrated or just plain angry, they are your feelings.

I never set out to ask people to change how they feel; my aim always is to look at what you can change in your behaviour. When you can change that in a positive way, then I can pretty much guarantee that your feelings will change as well.

Furthermore, just by trying something new, you will feel better because you will be breaking out of old, well-established patterns. Having said that, you might feel quite uncomfortable as you change your behaviour; your emotional self may well be taken aback that you've stepped out of the familiar and entered new territory.

Things to be aware of:

Be aware of what your home territory (where you are most 'at home') looks and feels like.

Be aware of how you change your behaviour when you're at family gatherings where you don't feel 'at home'.

Be aware of what your alien territory looks and feels like.

Be aware of the people you do care about and how you feel when you are with them.

Be aware of how that changes when you are with family members you don't like as much.

Things you could try:

If you were able to create a family sculpture, I'd like you to move someone who you've put at some distance to you much closer. See how that feels. Does it feel uncomfortable? Is this person one of those you yearn to be closer to? Do you want to put them right back where you started?

I'm still not suggesting you try anything out in the 'real world' just yet, but imagining making these changes is a good place to start.

To make genuine changes from family hell to family heaven, that's some of what will have to happen: how you are in relation to family members will have to change.

4

And Where Do You Fit In?

Good choices are made when you aren't in the throes of emotions. Most of us at some time or another have made decisions in the heat of the moment. Sometimes we regret them and can't or won't find a way to retract them. Sometimes we don't regret them, but there might still be a niggling feeling about whether the explosion was really necessary to achieve a good outcome.

Maybe walking away from some of your more stress-inducing family get-togethers is the right thing to do, but as I used to say to my psychotherapy clients, 'If you're going to walk away, walk away for the right reasons, not the wrong ones.' This means that instead of the usual knee-jerk reactions, you're going to have to make more considered choices if you want to change the get-together dynamic.

But before you can change it, you've got to know how you fit in, how you contribute to the family 'culture'. There are two things to look at here: one is to identify the patterns of behaviour in your family that get acted out when you get together; the second is to own up to what part you play in those patterns.

How does your knee jerk?

Let's begin first with what happens. If you look back to Chapter One at the family events you rated in the hell to heaven scale, pick a couple of the more disastrous ones for our next exercise.

At the hellish end of the scale family behaviour is relatively predictable; you most likely know who is going to say what; who will respond in what manner; what will happen next.

Case study: Tim's story continued

'I dread most of our family gatherings.

'As soon as I walk in the door, my mother accuses me of not visiting more often, and later my father will tell me how much I upset my mother. I get defensive and try to tell them how busy I am and that my weekends aren't that free.

'If my brother's around, of course, he'll say that he has a much more responsible job than I do and *he* always finds time to drop by. If he isn't there, one of my parents is sure to remind me of that fact anyway. "It's not as though you live a million miles away," they say.

'Now I'll feel as though everyone is ganging up on me and I go silent, shovel whatever food's put in front of me and afterwards slump in front of the telly (still silent) while my brother helps my mum do the washing-up.

'I feel like I'm in the middle of a soap opera and don't seem to be able to do anything about it.'

In Tim's case, everyone knows their parts well and have the same knee-jerk reactions to the same words.

This tends to be true with most family get-togethers that crowd the hellish end of the spectrum. We repeat and repeat behaviour, words and feelings just as though we were all handed a script beforehand and we've learned our lines well.

Exercise one

Reality checklist number one

There are many heavenly behaviours that even in family hell you and your family members may already do: things like showing empathy, tolerating differences of opinion, compromising gracefully, making sure problems are resolved. I'll be talking more about these behaviours and how you can achieve them later on.

However, right now I'm interested in helping you identify behaviours when things aren't going well; when family members aren't being understanding or tolerant or graceful. It is when families act out their negative patterns that trouble sets in and can get out of hand, making the family get-together so intolerable.

On pages 80–81 I've listed some of the more predictable behaviours that people do at their family get-togethers.

First, I'd like you to identify the ones you do and tick the appropriate boxes, and then the ones that you see other members of your family do.

Although I have described these as hellish behaviours, I'm not actually saying that any of them are wrong in and of themselves. Sometimes it's OK to demand things of our family; sometimes it's better to be conciliatory.

What I am interested in the context of this book is what you and your family do without thinking. That's what automatic behaviour is after all: we react without deliberation. We respond without consciously thinking about the impact our behaviour might have on others. Or we behave deliberately in order to create havoc with someone else. When I was little, I was an awful tattletale so I could get my older sister into trouble. Fortunately, I outgrew that in my teens, but all of us have the capacity to choose hellish behaviour just to get a rise out of another person. That's pretty knee-jerk, too.

I was chatting to one friend about this book and she said that one of the qualities that made her who she was, was her honesty and that it sometimes got her into trouble at family get-togethers, especially with her in-laws. As we discussed this, it was clear that her need to be honest was perhaps greater than her ability to see what the effect her honesty might have on others. She was still behaving in a knee-jerk way even if she was being true to herself.

Knee-jerk behaviour 'runs' us, we don't 'run' it, which means that we don't really choose our behaviour in these moments. Our reflexive reactions are in charge and we usually don't make very good choices at all.

Now. How honest were you with yourself? When you look at your reality checklist is it mostly others who do hellish behaviours? It usually is. When it comes to family I like to compare it to bad drivers: it's always the 'other guy' who's at fault, never ourselves. That's how we tend to react in emotional situations: 'I was really well-behaved, but you should have seen my uncle!'

This is completely understandable. It's often quite difficult to see our own behaviour as being anything other than 'right' when the people around us are behaving so 'wrong'. It will be one of the things I'm going to suggest you become more aware of at the summary of this chapter: to become more conscious of your own behaviour at your next few family get-togethers.

The more you understand what happens to you and your family, the better equipped you will be to do something about it.

It's also important to point out that even in very hellish families, there may be wonderful, loving and caring behaviours on display as well. I don't want to damn all families by saying hellish families are only ever hellish. They aren't. As we looked at in Chapter One, it isn't all bad and ugly – you probably will have identified some good in there as well. It's simply that under the pressure of unhappy family get-togethers a lot of that generous and thoughtful behaviour either gets lost in

Type of behaviour	You	Other family members
Be defensive		
Be conciliatory		
Get argumentative		
Go silent		
Hide in the kitchen/garden/etc.		
Arrive late		
Leave early		
Become bossy		
Start whingeing/whining		
End up crying		
Accuse others		
Start demanding		
Goad		
Tease		
Be too nice		
Become very reasonable		
Do anything for a peaceful life		
Gossip		
Tattletale		
Seethe		

Point score		
Side comment		
Walk out in a huff		
Take sides		
Criticise		
Finger point		
Cave in		
Back bite		
Please add any other behaviours you can think of that happen in your family that I might have missed off		

the turmoil or forgotten about as the more 'familiar' behaviour takes over.

I think it's worth taking a moment to give yourself a pat on the back for getting this far: personally, I find doing this work incredibly uncomfortable and, when I'm in the middle of it, I just want to run away and pretend it's everyone else's fault. I recommend a deep breath, a cup of tea (herbal or regular) and get ready for the next round.

Having looked at the behaviours you and your family do, it's now time to look at what goes hand in hand with behaviour: the roles people play.

When they handed out the scripts, what roles were you given?

The cause of many knee-jerk behaviours is due to the many roles that everyone takes on at some time or another in their families. Earlier I called myself the Human Buffer and the Rebel with a Cause. There are many, many more roles people take on and I've just scratched the surface with the list I've compiled over the years: these are the roles that exist in my and hundreds of other families I've known. They will be familiar to you.

As with behaviours, there's nothing intrinsically wrong with roles. However, when we play out these roles unconsciously, when we fall into them without thought or awareness of how they impact on others, that's when they can perpetuate the unhealthy dynamics in the family.

It is inevitable that when we enter alien territory, we take on roles that are less to do with our authentic selves and more to do with trying to create the family we want. The Human Buffer supposedly stops others from having a go at each other. As people in my family argued a lot, I grew up hating people arguing, so as an adult I set myself up to intervene when things got tough. I was once invited to a friend's family Christmas (very special, no outsiders had ever been included) because, as she said to me,

'They won't fight if you're there.' Ha, ha. They did.

That finally broke me of the habit I had fallen into of going along to other people's Christmases. When I first moved to the UK from America, my new friends said I couldn't possibly spend Christmas on my own so I went along to one family get-together after another for the first few years. I fell into playing the part of the Human Buffer even when it wasn't my family, and it didn't seem to do much good anyway.

Exercise two

Reality checklist number two

Roles are equally knee-jerk; we fall into them given the right circumstances. Even when we realise what we're doing, it can seem impossible to break the pattern.

Case study: Li's story

Li is 35, a doctor in a hospital in Germany, where her parents settled after leaving China in 1960.

'All my life I've felt a foreigner. I was born and brought up in Bonn, but my family have held on to traditional Chinese ways and always expect me and my siblings to do the same. We only speak Mandarin when we're together and my mother still doesn't speak German or any other language very well.

'The problem is I feel a foreigner at home as well. We're all expected to spend Sundays with my parents no matter what; it would be considered disrespectful if we didn't all come every week. Ma won't accept any help in the kitchen, even though my youngest brother and I love to cook, and Pa likes to sit back and watch his grandchildren play.

'But my kids and my other siblings' kids are getting to an age when they don't want to spend every Sunday trapped (as they see it) with a group of older people who don't understand what they're talking about.

'What happens is that Saturday morning, as soon as I wake up, I start getting nervous thinking about Sunday. I start worrying about what my kids might say to upset Grandpa; that my mother will criticise me for not teaching my children our language well enough; that my incredibly tolerant husband will finally lose his temper; that my eldest brother will make snide remarks to me and the rest of us siblings about how hopeless our parents are.

'By Sunday I'm completely on edge and start giving orders to everyone about how they are supposed to behave when we get to Grandpa's. I worry so much I lose my appetite and then of course Ma gets upset because she thinks I don't like her food.

'Between worrying and bossing my husband and kids around, I don't even recognise myself. At the hospital, I'm calm as a still lake no matter what the crisis, but put me with my family on an endless Sunday and I turn into somebody else.'

Li, like so many people, is stuck in the role she has played for a long time. Her sentiments are those I've heard many times: '. . . I turn into somebody else.' That's what roles do to us: they take over when we are under stress and we seem helpless to do anything about it.

It's the moment of truth. Turn to the table on pages 85–86. Like exercise one, tick the box next to the roles you know you play at times, then tick the ones that are familiar to you played out by others in your family.

And Where Do You Fit In?

Roles	You	Other Family Members
The Above It All . . . . . . distances him/herself from the fray because all the pettiness really has nothing to do with them		
The Accountant . . . . . . is especially adept at totting up hurts, insults, etc and is capable of presenting, at will, a complete balance sheet of who did what to whom		
The Arguer . . . . . . seems to take the opposite view, no matter what the topic		
The Black Sheep of the Family . . . . . . is the one everyone seems to have permission to talk about in derogatory terms		
The Bossy Boots . . . . . . tells everyone what to do and how to do it		
The Cataloguer . . . . . . is skilful at putting everyone in their 'place' and remembers hurts from prehistory		
The Cheerful One . . . . . . is relentlessly chirpy no matter what is going on		
The Conciliator . . . . . . is invariably trying to make things all right between people and often scurries from one person to another to resolve arguments		
The Confronter . . . . . . feels it's a good idea to get everything 'out in the open' and goes at everything head-on		

The Control Freak . . . . . . has to have everything done the way he/she thinks it ought to be done; can't bear it if anyone goes 'off piste'		
The Couch Potato . . . . . . takes up a position in front of the box and stays firmly planted there no matter what is happening around him/her		
The Doomsdayer . . . . . . always expects the worst and Cassandra-like predicts dire consequences, no matter what the situation		
The Door Slammer . . . . . . gets into rages and has to let everyone know how they feel by more than just leaving the room		
The Drama Queen/King . . . . . . has a life that always seems in crisis; some disaster has happened or is just about to happen		
The Feeling Squasher . . . . . . doesn't like to be around big emotions so makes jokes or snide remarks when others express how they feel		
The Flouncer . . . . . . seems to take offence easily and lets his/her feelings be known by exaggerated body language		
The Grown-up . . . . . . is terribly, terribly adult and treats other members of the family like little children		
The Human Buffer . . . . . . tries, by his/her very presence, to stop inevitable arguments (that'll be me, then . . .)		

And Where Do You Fit In?

The Hair-trigger . . . . . . flies of the handle at the slightest provocation		
The Invisible One . . . . . . melts away at the slightest sign of tension and keeps his/her head well below the parapet		
The Know-it-all . . . . . . sees what's best for everyone and has no compunction about letting everyone know just what that is		
The Long Suffering One . . . . . . tends to suffer in silence, except everyone knows about it		
The Marksman . . . . . . seems to know everyone's weak spots and often goes in for the kill		
The My Way or the Highway . . . . . . is big on making ultimatums		
The Negotiator . . . . . . similar to the Conciliator, but tries to make 'deals' between people		
The Open Wound . . . . . . suffers like no one else in the family and is finely attuned to the slightest hurts		
The Organiser . . . . . . likes to know that everyone has a job and makes sure everyone does it		
The Ostracised One . . . . . . is always on the outs with someone in the family and always feels an outcast		
The Placator . . . . . . is always trying to make it 'all right' for other people		

The Reasonable One . . . . . . is terribly rational and level-headed and comes up with 'reasonable' solutions no one is ever going to accept		
The Rebel With a Cause . . . . . . always has an important 'cause' he/she bangs on about, but also hides behind it (me again) . . .		
The Rebel Without a Cause . . . . . . doesn't have anything to hide behind but likes to stir things up just because . . .		
The Runner . . . . . . similar to the Door Slammer, he/she vanishes at the first sign of trouble or discord, or runs out in the middle of an argument		
The Sulker . . . . . . (we've all been here) is just like a stroppy teenager (indeed, may even be one) and feels sorry for him/herself because no one understands . . .		
The Talker . . . . . . babbles non-stop on just about anything, kind of like an endless stream of consciousness		
The Tearful One . . . . . . cries a lot, and often over seemingly inexplicable things		
The Troublemaker . . . . . . stirs things up between people and pits one person against another		
The Wayward One . . . . . . always seems to be in one form of trouble or another		

And where do you fit in?

The Whiner (Whinger) . . . . . . is never quite satisfied; things are never quite right, and everyone has to know about it		
The Worrier . . . . . . is a disaster monitor and is expert at making mountains out of molehills		
The Yeller . . . . . . is very loud and makes his/her points by screaming them		
Please add any that happen in your family that I might have missed off		

As with behaviours, roles, in and of themselves, are not 'wrong'. Everyone falls into some role or another at various times depending on whom they are with and what the circumstances are. However, within family dynamics those roles can be harmful, hurtful and serve simply to perpetuate the patterns that happen at family get-togethers.

In heavenly families people may also play roles – everyone is 'human' after all, but the impact of those roles is far less harmful because people are in charge of their behaviour, not the role. Also, in heavenly families there is a greater number of other, more positive behaviours and roles that people play out which offset the occasional lapse into thoughtless behaviour.

The difference is that these roles aren't covering up their genuine selves.

In hellish families, that's what happens: people take on roles to mask or distract from their deeper feelings of hurt, disappointment or longing.

Here is the key: we all have the capacity to choose the roles we want to play, and we all have the capability of breaking the negative cycle of knee-jerk behaviour.

Am I going to be stuck with these roles forever?

If looking over these lists makes you feel a bit queasy or embarrassed or uncomfortable, you're in the right place. You should be well on the way to building up a picture of how you interact with various members of your family and the impact this has on your family gatherings.

What do you suppose would happen if a few of you changed roles? What would happen if you, who might be the Open Wound, changed your role to become something completely different? As the Human Buffer and the Rebel with a Cause, everyone's quite used to my behaviour. What if I suddenly became the Tearful One or the Flouncer? It would shock everyone (myself included) and it would certainly change the family dynamic. Hard to think about, isn't it? How do you suddenly become the Whinger if you've always been the Silent One?

Exercise three

Part I

Because it is hard to change well-entrenched behaviours and roles, let's not start with any big changes just yet.

Together with my business partner, Robin Chandler, I run a company that creates workshops which are all about behavioural change. We often suggest to people that they change something simple in their home just to see what happens when they alter something they're used to. For instance, change the position of the rubbish bin or switch the underwear drawer with the sock drawer.

Try it. Try making a really simple but clear change and see what happens. One thing I can guess will happen is that you'll have a bunch of rubbish on the floor for a few days. Your hand will automatically go to the place the bin was before. In the same way, when you next go to put on your undies, you'll yank open the drawer that now holds socks and *then* you'll remember you switched the drawers.

If even changing your sock drawer seems too daunting, try something far simpler: move the icons on your computer around. The other day my computer hiccuped when I opened it and all the icons were in new spots. It took me a few minutes to realise that I was meticulously putting them all back to how they were, instead of leaving them be and seeing how long it would take me to get used to the new pattern.

It generally takes anywhere from a week or longer to stop automatically doing what you did before. And that's for easy stuff.

This will get you in the mood for the next level of practice, which is deliberately changing your behaviour because you want to.

Of course, changing something as simple as your underwear drawer or the icons on your computer is a lot easier that changing lifelong behaviour and patterns, especially when big feelings are attached to them. Anyone who's tried to give up a 'bad' habit (smoking, drinking too much alcohol, eating too many sweets, etc) knows just how difficult it is to make big changes. But if you really want to have a go at turning your family hells into family heavens, then change your behaviour is what you must do.

When you do change your behaviour, then things will change around you. The changes may not always be what you'd like or want, but whatever the outcome, it will be different from how things usually pan out, and that, of course, is what's needed if you are going to manage your family get-togethers more effectively.

Part II

Take a look at the list of behaviours and roles you've identified that you know (or suspect) that you do. Pick one that rings true to you; you know that when the family get-together gets rough, this is the behaviour and/or role you will invariably fall into without even thinking about it. Now, look at the list, at the behaviours and roles you haven't ticked, and choose one that's slightly different from your usual one and try to imagine what taking on that role would look and feel like. At this point, you're just trying to visualise some of the things you might say and do differently.

Case study: Anna's story continued

'What happened at my father's funeral is what always happens – my big brother got his way. Everyone was unhappy, in addition to being sad, except him, who didn't take any notice of how the rest of us were acting or how we might be feeling.

'After that I knew I had to do something or else I wouldn't be able to be in the same room with him again. The idea of changing roles felt really weird and I didn't think I'd be able to do it. At first it just didn't make sense.

'To begin with, I had to accept the idea that I was a placator. I never confront anyone in my family about anything – I'm the original people-pleaser. I knew I could never have a go at my brother so I'd have to choose something different, but I couldn't make it too different from my "normal" behaviour or I wouldn't be able to do it.

'I decided that because I never speak up it might be interesting to try to be a talker at the next family do, which was my younger brother's birthday.

'Right on cue, my older brother started telling everyone what to do. Normally, I'd be trying to make things OK for Mum, kind of staying in the background. I had decided ahead of time things I could talk about, and I just plunged right in and began talking and talking and talking; about what presents my brother was expecting, about the traffic, about global warming, about my niece's dance classes. It was great – once I started, I couldn't stop.

'At first everyone just looked at me, but it was strange because after a bit, my younger brother, his wife and Mum all began to talk a lot too. My older brother still bossed us around, but because we were all talking, no one seemed to mind that much; I certainly didn't.

'I think because I was doing something unusual for me, it felt really good and when he decided we should set the table in a certain way or hand out the slices of cake in a particular order, it just stopped being something to get upset about.'

What new role have you picked? Can you imagine some of the things you might say in this role? Can you imagine how others may react to you?

At this point, all I'm suggesting is that you think about taking on a different role. I'll give you another couple of steps before I suggest you take this change into the 'dragon's den'.

The first part of this exercise is to show you what happens when you make even the smallest changes in your routine. It's not necessarily that easy. Or even if it's easy, you will still have tiny moments of forgetting you've made any change and revert to how things used to be, whether it's where you've placed the rubbish bin, or the order in which you hang up your shirts or blouses.

For my own mini-experiment while writing this book, I moved my in tray from the left side of my desk to the right side. My desk is not big – I can easily see the in tray on the right – and yet I automatically put the bills and letters on the left side without even thinking about it. For a while, I had an empty in tray and a pile of loose papers on the other side of the desk.

If we have involuntary reactions to even the smallest changes, then changing actual behaviour based on strong emotions is not necessarily going to be easy, which is why I've suggested just imagining taking on a new role for the time being.

Resistance

Often, our biggest resistance to changing our behaviour is our fear of how others will react. I'll be going into far more detail about this in Chapters Five and Eight, but it's worth noting now just what your reactions are to even the thought of changing what you do at your family gatherings.

We're concerned that we'll hurt people's feelings, that we'll be rejected, that we'll never be forgiven, that we won't be accepted. Any of that might indeed happen.

However, our imaginings are usually far worse than the reality. So for the time being, simply note (in a journal, in your head, to a friend) how you feel when you think about any changes you might make in the roles that you play.

Can I hand back the script, please?

If it wasn't so awful at times, it would be funny. Have you ever noticed how during a particularly hellish family get-together everyone speaks (or yells) as though they're auditioning for a melodrama or they're repeating words and phrases they've heard off the TV?

Clichés abound and the words really do seem scripted. The words may be heartfelt but they often don't feel as though they're coming from the heart, rather they sound as though some hack playwright made them up.

Such as:

'If you're not going to consider my feelings, fine then.'

'You never take into account what I want.'

'Just what are you implying?'

'Will everyone just stop picking on me.'

'Why is it always me who has to make the decisions?'

'If I've told you once, I've told you a hundred times; I don't eat potatoes. Why do you insist on putting them on my plate?'

'All this arguing is doing my head in. Would all of you just please stop?'

'What did I say? Did I say anything that was so bad?'

'You're being oversensitive.'

'Come on, stop crying. Let me see a smile. Come on, I'm sure you have a little smile in there for me.'

'Stop telling me what to do.'

'You never bother to understand what I'm trying to say.'

'How dare you speak to me like that.'

'It's not fair. Why am I always the one who has to be responsible?'

'Here we go again.'

I was writing those 'lines' in an arbitrary order, using ones I've heard in my own family or that others have told me. But when I read them back to myself it seemed as though they could almost be a scene from a play, couldn't they? They're full of emotions but no one's really saying anything new. It's like eating popcorn – it may feel good going down, but it's purely empty calories. There are lots of words but not a lot of meaning. As a matter of fact, I think I'll call them popcorn statements, and I'll be referring to them again in future chapters.

Actually, the phrases are communicating quite a bit of meaning, it's just all hidden.

Take the potato line, for instance:

'If I've told you once, I've told you a hundred times; I don't eat potatoes. Why do you insist on putting them on my plate?'

What could be going on might be any of the following. . .

'What I really want is for you to notice that I'm trying to eat a healthy diet and potatoes just don't figure on the menu.'

'I wish you'd stop serving mountains of food and sit and talk to me for a bit.'

'I find it really difficult to give up my Friday evenings to be with you, when I'd rather be out with my mates.'

. . . or any of 800 different things.

The point is that the use of clichés and scripted lines usually means there's something else going on underneath. It may not necessarily be appropriate to say what's underneath, but until the script gets changed, you have no hope of changing the family dynamics.

To do that, you've got to get conscious about how everyone's lines feeds the current family dynamic.

Exercise four

Here we're going to look at some of the players and the scripts. Be as honest as possible when looking at your family from this perspective.

Every family has a hierarchy. By this I mean the person who holds the 'power' in the family. It may not be the official 'head' of the family. It may not always be the person who yells the loudest or is the bossiest. It can be the quiet one who stops people from arguing with a single glance, or it can be the 'baby' of the family to whom everyone caters. It can be the stroppy teenager everyone is afraid of and tiptoes around, or it can be the one who's making a mint at their job. Hierarchy also isn't about who's the eldest, the youngest, middle child, or whether you're an only, a twin or one of a dozen. Although many books, articles and websites have been written about how 'birth order' can shape your personality, I am less interested in how you got to be how you are, and far more interested in how you behave today with your family members.

Part I

Hierarchy

1. Who's top of the heap in your family hierarchy?

____

2. Where do you fit in the pecking order?

____

3. Who (if anyone) are you most intimidated by?

____

4. Who do you get on with well?

____

5. Is it easier when there are a lot of you together, or when just a few?

____

Family Sculpting revisited

If you think back to the Family Sculpture you did (or thought about), I'd like you now to redo your sculpture in terms of the hierarchy of the family. Take those objects (or drawing or talking to a friend) and place them in relation to each other in terms of the family hierarchy. Is there any difference?

I also know that for many of us, things do change when talking one to one with family members than when there's a whole gang. My older sister and I are pretty open with each other when we're alone, but put us in a family group and she clams up and barely says a word (oops, I lost my ally there!). Whereas, with another of my siblings there's no real difference when we're on our own or in the larger mix.

I'd like you to see where/if there's a difference in your behaviour when you are one to one with certain members of your families as opposed to when you're in a group.

Behaviour

6. Thinking about the person you are most intimidated by in your family, how do you behave differently (if you do behave differently) when you are with him/her one to one or in a group?

____

____

____

____

7. Thinking about the person you get on with really well, how (if you do) do you behave differently with him/her one to one or in a group?

The Script

On many occasions just about everyone communicates with his or her family from scripts that have been repeated before and before that. Taking one of your recent family get-togethers, see if you can answer the next few questions.

8. Can you identify some of the 'lines' family members say over and over again?

9. What might be underneath some of these lines?

10. Can you identify some of the 'lines' you say over and over again?

11. What's underneath some of your lines?

It might be time for another deep breath and a break. Looking beneath the surface of our behaviour and words can be hard work. This kind of process can stir up lots of feelings and thoughts and memories, so you need to pace yourself to what you are comfortable with – you don't have to do it all in one go.

Exercise five

This is for those of you feeling particularly brave. Alternatively, you can think about it and return to it later when you are feeling more confident.

Can you take the plunge?

It's time to try it out; to try practising a new and different role at your next family get-together.

First, choose your new role. It can be the same one you chose in exercise three, the one you visualised trying out, or it can be another, completely different one. I'm going to suggest you 'rehearse' taking on the new role before you make your debut at the next family event. If you have a good and trusted friend, instead of moaning to them about the up-and-coming gathering (most of us are guilty of this particular behaviour), why not try practising on them first. It's not as silly as it sounds.

Considering you already have a ready-made script in your head when you fall into one of your knee-jerk roles, why not prepare a script ahead of time with some new lines? Practising outside the line of fire is a wise move – and this is true when trying out any new behaviour, whether it has to do with your family or not.

When you have a handle, or think you do, on this new role, the next thing to do is be a bit calculated about how and when you're going to use it. I wouldn't suggest you rush in and try it first thing. Having looked at some of the scripts that go on in your family, you should have a pretty good idea of when your lines come in, so there shouldn't be too much difficulty in pre-planning what you might do differently and when. You might decide that just introducing this new role or new behaviour once is enough.

Good. You gave it a try and once may be more than enough on the first go. Actually, I say 'good' even if all you've done is to identify your behaviour and roles without trying out anything new. With increased awareness, your family get-togethers aren't going to look the same anyway.

Gradually, as you follow the plan of this book – even if you don't initially do any of the exercises with your family – things will begin to change. You can't undo awareness, and once insight grabs hold of you, it becomes more and more difficult to hang on to unhelpful behaviours.

Case study: Morris's story continued

'I really fought the idea that there was anything in what I did that wasn't OK. It was very hard for me to admit that maybe I played any kind of role when I was with my mother and sister.

'It really did seem as though it all had to do with the two of them, but after this past New Year I realised that whenever I saw them whispering together I became over-the-top jolly. I cracked jokes, I would even do pratfalls (at 62!). What I realised I was doing, of course, was trying to get their attention and I've been doing that all my life.

'What bothered me was that I realise I do that with friends at work. Whenever I think other people are having a better time than me or getting on better with each other than they are with me, I crack jokes and talk loudly and become the life and soul of the party.

'On your advice I chose a different role; I decided to try to become invisible. I know you said to try something close to what I normally do, but I decided to up the stakes and do just the opposite.

'Oh, brother. They didn't even notice! I sat there (all 200 lbs of me) trying to shrink into the sofa, and they just carried on like I wasn't there.'

It might not work! It might backfire. You could go into the 'dragon's den' and get mauled. Or, like Morris, no one will notice and it will seem like a wasted effort. It won't be.

Variation on a theme

If you haven't been able to pick a role to try out, here's another approach with which to have a go: try choosing the *opposite* behaviour to one of your regular roles. For instance, as the Human Buffer, I'm often caught between opposing 'camps' and my behaviour will be about ameliorating people's conflicts with each other or at the very least hoping my very presence might stop others from acting out (ha, ha). In retrospect, I can see now that there were situations where, if I had done absolutely nothing, I would have been better off. Since my human buffering didn't do much good, the person who suffered most was me.

The opposite of the Human Buffer would be the Withdrawer perhaps, and in some situations that's what might take care of me, even if it doesn't resolve the actual situation.

So think about it: if you're a Doomsdayer, you could try to be someone who only looks for the positive in any situation that arises; if you're the Reasonable One, have a go at being Unreasonable. It would certainly make a change and you never know what the results might produce.

The important thing is to choose.

Remember, good choices are made when you aren't in the throes of emotion. When you make conscious choices an interesting thing happens. Although your heart may beat faster, your palms may get sweaty and your throat may go dry, believe it or not, you will feel less emotional. When you do knee-jerk, automatic, unthinking behaviour, you are reacting to what is happening around you. When you choose your behaviour you will be in charge and you will be engaging your brain before your mouth.

Things to be aware of:

Be aware of the hierarchy in your family and how you behave within that hierarchy.

Be aware of your knee-jerk behaviour when you get together with your family.

Be aware of the roles you and your family members play.

Be aware of the 'scripts' you all speak from.

Be aware of the hidden meanings that might lie beneath the scripts.

Things you could try:

Try making some really small changes in what you do, like moving the rubbish bin, or taking a different route to and from work or to do the shopping. Notice if your first instinct is to do the old pattern and how long it takes you to adapt to a new one.

Choose a different role to play at your next family gathering. If you have a difficult time choosing a new role, choose the behaviour that's opposite your normal role. Try it out on a friend first.

If you don't feel up to using that new role with your family, when you're next with them, try saying some new words in your head – what you might say if you were playing that role.

5

Bullseye from 15 Paces – Charting Your Personal 'Family-o-gram'

Still hanging in there?

How are you doing so far? This kind of self-development work isn't always easy and anything to do with families is generally fraught with bigger emotions than usual. It certainly is for me. So far most of the suggestions I've made have been about perception, raising your awareness and thinking about what it might feel like if you make changes. Whenever you take on new ways of behaving there has to be a firm foundation of understanding so that what you do makes sense in the context of your own life.

This chapter has even more awareness raising about your family dynamics, but it's time to start doing things out in the field now – changes you can begin to make at your family get-togethers. Small, doable steps is the way I am able to put changes in place, and is certainly what I recommend you do.

Now it's time to look in more detail at your family patterns, rules, what gets your goat and whose goat you get.

Quack, quack

Sitting ducks, most of us. It won't take much to set us off with our mothers, brothers, uncles, cousins. Family members seem to be particularly adept at point scoring, feather ruffling and other sure-fire techniques guaranteed to rile. As I pointed out in Chapter Two, there are family members who can do things that we tolerate, perhaps not even notice as niggling or annoying. Yet, someone else who gets our goat can do the same thing and we're irritated beyond belief. They seem to have an uncanny ability to figure out what's going to upset us the most and they go for the jugular: it seems as though they deliberately wind us up.

I'm 100 per cent certain that in many family get-togethers people are indeed deliberately winding each other up. And guess what? We all do it, too. We aren't just the recipients of someone else's sharp tongue or sarcastic dig; all of us have, and will have used, the ability to get our own back, slip in the caustic word, the sceptical look, the raised eyebrow of disbelief.

Why? It's a very powerful place to be, to see that our little asides, toss-away lines and well-aimed barbs can have quite an impact. I already told you that when I was younger I liked nothing better than to get my older sister into trouble if I could. I was quite happy to see if I could get at her and really be as annoying as possible, and she did it right back, tit for tat. All of us siblings did it to each other at some point, some more than others, depending upon who we were most angry with on any particular day. We each had our favourites; whoever we got on better with had the good fortune of not being a target. Teasing with intent is what I call it.

We all have teasing techniques guaranteed to get someone's goat and really annoy them. From quite an early age we learn them and carry them on straight into adulthood. Oh, maybe not the exact same techniques; we will have refined them. So not only do we get our knees jerked, most of us are pretty adept at jerking our family members' knees as well.

There's a technique that many, if not most, children use at some time or another that's absolutely guaranteed to bring out the monster in most people. That's the mimicking one. You know it (you may even have done it yourself) . . . you say something and they say it right back to you with a slight change in the tone of voice. It escalates and you've been 'got' again by someone a sixth your age:

You, being stern: 'Jenny, you have to get ready for school.'

She, with a whiny tone: 'Jenny, you have to get ready for school.'

You, getting sterner: 'Don't give me that backchat, get dressed.'

She, getting whinier: 'Don't give me that backchat, get dressed.'

You, beginning to fray at the edges: 'I'm warning you.'

She, really enjoying herself: 'I'm warning you.'

You, having lost it: 'If you don't get dressed right now, you'll have to stay in after school, and that's final.'

She will now be making a decision just how far to push you.

I know I shouldn't be surprised, because not a lot does surprise me, but I am amazed that this particular wind-up seems to be universal and is used by children all over the globe. It's as though there is a collective unconscious of 'designed-to-really annoy' skills that children pick up and use with great glee.

Well, that glee carries right over into adulthood and though the techniques might be marginally more sophisticated, the results are often the same: certain people will be able to get you no matter how well armed you think you are, and you could very well fray at the edges and lose it.

Case study: Anina's story

'Ah, *ma famiglia*! We're a very close-knit Italian family; typical, I guess you could say. We're volatile, affectionate, love to eat big meals, are in and out of each other's houses. Any excuse for a party: anniversaries, birthdays, Liberation Day, Ferragosto, Easter, Christmas – we go all out and the more, the merrier.

'Except for my older brother. He needles me the way no else can. He gets under my skin and I find my blood boiling when we start our constant snipes at each other. It came to a head one Christmas Eve recently – the whole family was there as usual – my kids, his kids (all teens at this point). We're sitting down to the huge meal my mother always cooks (with help from the other women in the family, but it's Mama's day to shine), and Michele and I begin.

'Back and forth as we go just as we have always done, seeing who could shove the other hardest. We're not even sitting all that close to each other so we have to raise our voices every time we go to score a point. Meanwhile, everyone seems to be ignoring us since they're used to it (or so I thought), and they're chatting and eating, passing huge dishes of stuffed trout, cappelletti, *melanzane parmigiano*, chestnut-stuffed capon, bowls of roasted vegetables.

'I decide (unconsciously, I have to add feebly in my defence) to ratchet up the guerrilla fighting and without even thinking I say, "Michele, why don't you just go out and slit your throat?" He gets up from the table and storms out and I carry on eating, while everyone else has now stopped and is looking at me accusingly and Papa is trying to calm it all down.'

Nil, nil

Anina's story isn't unusual. In every family people will be point scoring off each other, except, of course, no one really wins, however momentarily satisfying it may be when you hit the bullseye.

I became much happier when I began to have a proper relationship with my older sister, rather than either avoiding her or figuring out ways of getting at her. I was fiercely jealous of her so trying to score points off her was my way of making her pay.

Case study: my story

I once found a particularly effective way of getting my older sister into trouble, which was my main aim when I was a little kid. I could only have been three or four, she would have been six or seven. My mother popped out quickly and left Beth in charge. Not a good idea.

She pissed me off in some way, so I figured I'd get my own back. I got myself dressed completely, snuck out the front door, walked carefully down the five flights of stairs and took myself to the corner drugstore where they had stacks of books and comics on a stand. I settled down to read and completely lost track of time (as you do when you're three).

I was discovered by my mother, the friend she was with and Beth and a resultant fuss was made.

Was I in trouble for running off? No, there was simply relief I was so easily (and predictably) found. Did I get my sister into trouble? I don't think so, but I was completely satisfied with the effect I had had on everyone. What a powerful place to be and I honed my skills over the years to try to alleviate my jealousy.

It just occurred to me that in order to get my sister into trouble I had to raise my own game since I had never got dressed completely on my own at that age, nor had I ever taken myself off on my own, down five flights of stairs, into the street and into a shop where I made myself invisible enough to be ignored by the shopkeeper. Another Jo Ellen insight! I just realised that this is a pattern I do in my life: I continually raise my game, give myself what looks like impossible challenges, stretch my capabilities. And I'm still doing it.

I'll be getting to your lifetime patterns in a few pages, but first I want to continue the point-scoring theme for a while.

In Chapter Two, I asked you to make a list of people you don't get on with all that well in your family and what they do that gets up your nose. Well, now I'm going to ask you to do just the opposite.

Them and us

Have you noticed that most of the time (nearly every time?) something upsetting happens at one of your family get-togethers, it's generally someone else's fault? Like the wish lists in Chapter Two and the roles in Chapter Four, it's so much easier to look at what other people have to change in order to make things better, how others play difficult or annoying roles, how others wind us up and make the family get-togethers hellish. This is completely understandable. It does seem to be the 'way we're made'. Even in the heavenly families I know, it seems much easier to point the finger to someone 'over there' who's causing all the trouble.

Fred, who has been doing all the exercises in this book and gaining loads of personal insights about his own family dynamics still calls someone in the family (who shall remain nameless), the Axis of Evil. He still can't let go of his resentments or accept the fact that it can't all be the other person's fault. With thinking like this, the dynamics between certain family members will remain 'them' and not 'us'.

Now's the time to take the plunge and look at just whose nose you get up. Who do you point score against? What do you do that makes other people's blood boil? When are you the 'them'?

Exercise one

If you're anything like me, at first I struggle to identify who I might annoy, frustrate, anger. I'm uncomfortable with the idea that anything in the unhealthy family dynamics has anything to do with me. I'm innocent while they are guilty. Not true, of

Who	What do you do that gets up their nose?

course; we all contribute to the family dynamics in the same way as we all have roles we play.

Fill in the table above. Are the people who get up your nose the same people whose noses you get up? I ask that because, like Anina, there may be individuals in your family with whom you have a mutual point-scoring relationship. Then again, there may very well be people who you quite like, but you do things that really annoy the hell out of them. You may resist admitting it, but once we reach adulthood no one is completely innocent when it comes to difficulties in the family.

Exercise two

Think about a recent hellish family get-together and identify where you were 'them'; where you possibly could have been the 'culprit' and done something that someone else didn't like. There's no right or wrong here, no need to justify whatever it was you did. I'd simply like you to spot those times when your behaviour will have been looked on by someone else as inappropriate or annoying or embarrassing, etc. Did you know you were doing it at the time? In other words, was it unconscious or deliberate, calculated, retaliating?

In reviewing what happened, is there anything at this point you think you could have done differently? Don't worry if there isn't.

Play it again, Sam

It's clear that we can get 'got', and that we can 'get' others. Most of us have more complex family relationships than ever before; we all play roles; we have unfulfilled wishes; we can feel in alien territory. We can have jolly good times and hellish times.

Most of all, whatever it is we do, it won't be the first time: we are the result of patterns, beliefs and rules that get repeated over and over again. Things that others do provoke a reaction in us, and things we do provoke reactions in others.

Every family, wherever they are, has spoken and unspoken rules. Rules are not bad things at all. It gets interesting only when someone 'disobeys' or rebels against the family rule structure.

Every family is different and the dynamics in each one will be unique to the people in it. I used the term 'culture clash' in an earlier chapter, and in a way you could say that every family has its own unique culture separate from any formal national, religious or racial culture.

Case study: Cheryl's story

Cheryl is 40, a homemaker, living in large Lincolnshire village with three young children of her own.

'I come from a really big family: three brothers and two sisters. My dad sometimes has to go through the whole list of us before he gets to the right name when he's talking to one of us.

'We have bucket-loads of aunts and uncles and cousins and we're continually going to weddings, christenings and birthday parties.

> 'When someone new joins the family we say "innocent until proven guilty". In other words, you're all right until you do something that upsets the family. Then you better watch out because hurt one of us, you hurt us all.
>
> 'The funny thing is, it hardly happens at all. Maybe newcomers feel that bond and realise they'll be on to a hiding to nothing if they try to take us on. Whatever, it seems to work.'

A bit tribal, that, but it certainly seems to work for them.

Wherever you go in the world people are people and the way they behave at family get-togethers is a reflection of their family culture as well as their national, religious or racial one. The roles and rules in the majority of families are more powerful than just about anything else.

Here's a simple one from my family. We were all brought up with a very clear rule that no one started to eat until everyone in the family was sitting at the table. This was for every meal, whether a special event or not. It's ingrained. I cannot go anywhere and not follow that rule, and for a long time I found it peculiar, if not downright rude, that everyone else didn't do the same.

I can remember the first time I went to someone else's house for a meal and was genuinely shocked when family members began to tuck in before everyone was gathered. Shocked and, in my self-righteous little way, disapproving as well. They weren't following the rules. I am not making a value judgement now (though I certainly did then) about whether my family rule was right and this family's rule was wrong. The point is that I came up against a clash of rules and it bothered me. To tell the truth, it still bothers me a little when this happens, no matter how much I'm urged to 'Start without me.'

That's one small rule out of about a zillion in my family. It's also an example of a spoken rule, the kind that got drummed into me as I was growing up. What about the unspoken ones?

The ones we all consciously or, more likely, unconsciously, pick up from our families. These rules, I believe, are far more insidious because they aren't talked about, but if you break one of them, there will surely be consequences.

An unspoken rule in my family was never to talk about the big stuff. Big stuff, of course, was anything that had to do with how we really felt about . . . anything. Small stuff might trigger very big arguments, but it was the stuff underneath the arguments that never saw the light of day. No one ever told any of us not to discuss important emotional issues, we just knew not to. That was an unspoken rule that in many instances is still adhered to. Easier to fight over inconsequential things than to go where the deep hurts lie.

Once again let me add that many unspoken rules aren't bad – many things that were taken for granted in my family were positive and helpful. It's only in the context of unhealthy family patterns that unspoken rules can be damaging. In the context of family get-togethers these unspoken rules gain even more power and influence.

Many of the rules in my family – spoken and unspoken – are now so firmly entrenched that I don't even know they're rules; they simply feel, 'Well, that's just me; that's who I am.'

There will be rules in your family as well. If not a rule, it may be a pattern – things you and your family do because you've always done them that way. Just as I described in Chapter Four, we all have patterns of behaviour – our roles – that are hard to change. Rules become patterns, which in turn become beliefs, usually hard and fast ones.

In other words, I'm brought up with the rule that everyone has to be seated before the meal can begin, it becomes a well-ingrained pattern till it eventually becomes a belief: NO ONE in *any* family, *anywhere,* should begin eating till everyone is seated at the table.

That's all well and good as long as I'm with people who agree with my rule, but what happens when someone new comes into the family who doesn't have that rule? Trouble ahead. That new in-law or long-lost cousin or stepdaughter suddenly becomes rude, thoughtless and inconsiderate in light of how the family functions. They didn't actually do anything wrong, except break a rule they didn't even know existed. The patterns and rules in families are like bear pits; unsuspecting people fall into them without having a clue what they've done wrong.

Introducing the 'family-o-gram'

OK, so what's a family-o-gram?

Among psychotherapists and health practitioners there's this neat tool called a genogram. It can get very complicated, but the idea is that it's a type of family tree to help you track family health and relationship patterns such as cancer, divorce, alcoholism, etc. Genograms tend to go back at least three generations or more if at all possible (I remember many years ago I did a genogram with a client who had a long history of murder and mysterious deaths on both sides of the family – yikes!) and in psychotherapy I occasionally used it to help clients identify what patterns they might be perpetuating without even realising it. Genograms use a collection of symbols, colour-coded lines and different kinds of 'legends' to depict emotional and social relationships. They are way too complicated for this book, though if you want to go very deep into your family's history they are a very good tool and there's lots of software to help you create a multilevel picture of your background.

I'm interested in a simpler family tree which I've called a family-o-gram; one that looks at current relationships and behaviour patterns at family get-togethers. Patterns do get repeated intergenerationally (in other words, they get passed down from one generation to another), and if you have a good understanding you might be able to track some of these patterns back more than one or two generations. If you don't, just looking at the current behaviour patterns will work just as well.

Case study: my story continued

As I mentioned earlier, in one part of my family, we have that terrific pattern of door-slamming and running out. Shortly after my stepmother died in hospital, two of my siblings disappeared and, when the rest us of got back to the house with my very upset father, we had no idea where they had gone. They didn't phone in to tell us where they were or when they'd get back.

Hours later they returned and my father wanted to know where they'd been – he had wanted his whole family around him. I did my Human Buffer thing – big mistake. A shouting match ensued with the aforementioned door slamming and then re-vanishing for a time. Since then there are now cliques of siblings who don't talk to each other. It's as though they are still 'vanished'.

Even my father got caught up in a silent treatment breach with his beloved brother quite late in their lives. I don't know what actually happened, all I do know is that it took my stepmother's death notice for my uncle to heal the rift by showing up at the house carrying a big box of pastries the day after she died.

I'm used to this, however, as this is an intergenerational pattern being carried on in the best traditions of maintaining a dysfunctional status quo: my stepmother at various times didn't speak to her sister or her brother, and they all died without there ever being a reconciliation.

She, in turn, would get angry at various ones of us from quite early childhood (mine, I mean, not hers) and there would be many times when one of us would be given the silent treatment till we figured out what kind of apology would make it better. This carried on throughout our adult lives as well – generally, there was one of us she wasn't speaking to at one point or another, because that was the way she had learnt to deal with her distress, anger, disappointment.

> So the pattern continues with my siblings, who also use silence as a way of expressing their uncomfortable feelings.
>
> But it can get a bit explosive at our family gatherings where feelings are more exposed and all of our differences are more apparent.

One thing I know can happen is that when we grow up in difficult families we often vow we won't let it happen when we get into relationships. We won't let history repeat itself for yet another generation. Good try, but though it's not always true, very often we are attracted to people who will fit right in with our patterns and rules so when they join the family there will be a match even if that wasn't our intention.

Like Cheryl's family, your family dynamic may be made of many rules that an outsider would defy at their peril.

Let's take a look at some more things that happen in your family.

Exercise three

Your family-o-gram

You can do this so that it looks like a family tree, just write it out in list form or even just think about it. The important thing is to look at your family from a behaviour pattern point of view. Start simple, with the obvious and most likely the more you do, the more you'll think of.

Your family-o-gram

Paternal Grandparents

Maternal Grandparents

Aunts

Uncles

Father

Mother

Aunts

Uncles

Siblings

Siblings

Self

Children

Children

Children

Children

Children

It looks like a family tree, doesn't it?

Here's the difference between a family tree and a family-o-gram: rather than dates of births, deaths and marriages, I'd like you to list in each of the boxes characteristics, patterns and rules that you associate with each person. Take a look at the relationships you have with various family members and add them in. Be sure to include anyone outside your blood (or adopted) family: in-laws, new wives' children, etc. You may need to add extra boxes depending on how complex your 'cocktail' is. Be sure to include who you get on with, who you don't and why. See if you can write down the nature of the arguments you have, or if you don't argue, the nature of your resentments or frustrations.

This might be a good time to take the roles you identified in Chapter Four and add them to the boxes as well, to see if any interesting patterns emerge. If you're finding this bit somewhat tricky, just go back to one of your recent hellish family get-togethers and just write down what happened and with whom. Then see if that triggers any other patterns or rules. You might need bigger boxes!

After you've filled it in or made your lists or thought about it, see if you can identify any patterns – like mine with the silent treatment. Hold on to these – we'll be doing something with them in a few minutes.

It may be that you can't attach a specific person to a specific rule that either you follow or most people in your family follow, so make a separate Rules of the game list.

Rules of the game

Cliché though it may be, a lot of the relationships we have with family members are all about game playing. And the games seem to get magnified at family gatherings.

All games have rules. Ever watch little children at play? I'm talking about the four-, five- or six-year-old range, perhaps even older.

Children make up the rules of whatever game they're playing whether or not they make sense to the adults who might be eavesdropping. The rules make sense to the children. I think of family game playing as a bit like that: somewhere along the line, the rules got made up and everyone follows them whether they make sense or not. Except they do make sense to the particular family.

Let me say again, this isn't about judging whether these are 'good' rules or 'bad' ones. The thing about the power of rules is to look at whether they run you or you run them. Like the roles you identified, are they knee-jerk or do you really think about them? My 'everyone-has-to-be-sitting-at-the-table' rule is totally knee-jerk. It doesn't matter whether I or any one else thinks it's good manners, this is a rule that 'runs' me. It's a pattern that it would be hard for me to break.

Here are some rules (spoken and unspoken) and patterns I've heard over the years and, of course, since talking to people about this book, many have been quick to share theirs with me:

Everyone fights over the tab (if we're at a restaurant or pub) every single time, even though we know what the outcome is going to be.

We women congregate in the kitchen while our men plop in front of the TV or hover over the barbecue. We women then complain about the men not helping but they'd just be underfoot anyway, so we'd rather they didn't come into the kitchen at all. But we still like to complain – it's part of the pattern now.

Everyone is expected to contribute equally to presents for our parents no matter what our individual incomes are.

No one contradicts my father – ever.

My children have to ask permission before they leave the table.

At Christmas, everyone opens one present at a time in turn, so there always has to be an equal number of presents for everyone so no one feels left out. This means if someone has fewer presents than the others, someone has to go out and get more.

There always has to be enough food on the table before people arrive, no matter how many are expected.

As soon as my father comes home from work, everyone stops what they're doing and we sit down to dinner immediately.

Whenever there's a family do at one of our houses, everything has to be cooked from scratch, no ready-made meals or takeaways are allowed.

Whenever anyone visits anyone else in the family, we always have to bring something, no matter how often we might see each other.

No kissing or hugging in my family.

Notice how many rules there are around food and eating. There were a lot more I didn't include, but that was a pattern with nearly everyone I spoke to. There seems to be a lot of expectations of how family members are supposed to behave when it comes to food. I assume that's because so many family get-togethers do centre around meals, parties or celebrations. And when a family get-together is heavenly there is nothing in my mind as convivial, warm and inviting as sitting around with people I love 'breaking bread' and sharing delicious food.

However, there are loads of rules that don't have to do with food as well. You and your family will have loads of rules as well.

Exercise four

What are some of the spoken and unspoken rules in your family?

____

____

____

____

____

How do they play themselves out at family gatherings?

____

____

____

____

____

Exercise five

In the last chapter, I suggested that you pick one of your usual roles and change it at the next family get-together. I'm upping the stakes now, and suggesting that you overturn one of the rules your family plays by.

Let's take one of the rules from the list, the one about there always has to be food laid out no matter how many people are expected. According to my suggestion, in order to overturn the rule, there would have to be no food laid out, no extra stocks in the kitchen. The first thing that might happen is that everyone would be surprised. If they're used to going to, say, 'Aunt Jane's' house and there's *always* a lovely spread on the table, they'd wonder just what was going on. Was Aunt Jane all right? Was something going on that they needed to know about?

Something different would then have to happen. Aunt Jane's family might ignore the empty table and carry on as though nothing was different. Someone might suggest getting a takeaway or going out for lunch. Someone could go shopping and cook the meal themselves.

A pattern would have been disrupted, expectations would be disappointed. Maybe family visitors would be relieved because they always feel guilty at all the trouble Aunt Jane goes to. Or maybe they never liked her food anyway. Maybe everyone will be disappointed and feel neglected.

When a rule is broken, you don't know what the consequences will be.

What would happen if the person who had the rule about bringing something every time they visited broke it and came empty-handed? Would the host be offended? If you were the person with the rule would you feel uncomfortable, awkward, out of place without something in your hand? Would you feel ungenerous and mean? I don't know what would happen and neither will you.

If I just dig in to the meal the next time I'm with my family, I expect it will feel extremely weird, uncomfortable, rude and just plain against the grain. So I think I better try it! As I'm writing this, I'm imagining if anyone will notice or whether everyone will notice.

You try it. Pick a rule and imagine what your reaction will be to breaking the rule and what you imagine other family members' reactions might be. The biggest impediment to changing behaviour is what we make up in our heads. I know; I have spent endless amounts of time wondering what other people's reaction might be if I did something or said something out of the 'norm'. I'm fairly courageous when it comes to saying things and yet I will still have those discussions in my head about what might happen. I expect that you, too, will have long intense discussions in your head about how others might react to you doing things differently.

Even so, try it. The outcome may not be what you expect or even desire, but it will mean you are doing something to change the patterns at your family get-togethers.

They won't like it

That's usually the first reaction I hear when I suggest people try changing one of their rules. Actually, it's the second thing I hear. The first is usually 'I couldn't possibly do that.'

I mentioned resistance before. When we start challenging well-entrenched patterns of behaviour, it is common to think we just can't do it.

Sometimes we react strongly because we come up against a whole set of beliefs. Asking Aunt Jane not to prepare food for the multitudes may test her beliefs about hospitality, generosity, other people's expectations, it's what she's always done, why should she stop now, and so on. Just as asking me not to wait till everyone is sitting will come up against my beliefs about looking after everyone, politeness, having a shared experience.

This isn't about questioning your beliefs or even asking you to discard them or modify them. It is to see whether you can start changing the family patterns that you know contribute towards creating hellish family get-togethers.

'They' may not like it. 'They' may be horrified at your behaviour. 'They' might not notice (remember poor Morris, who tried changing one of his roles in the last chapter – no one noticed any change at all). 'They' might wonder what's come over you. You don't know. You won't know till you try. That sounds just like something I heard when I was a child, 'It won't kill you. Try it, you won't know until you try it.' You won't know until you try.

Case study: Silvio's story continued

'I never thought about rules when it comes to my family, but I have lots. Talking about what happened when Alberto was born, I realise that there were a lot of rules going on.

Like my parents *should* give me the same things as they gave my brother and sister. Like they *should* offer, I *shouldn't* have to ask.

'I made up all those rules and I can see now that I got angry at everyone for not obeying my rules. The hardest thing I've done in a long time was to break one of my own rules, the one about I *shouldn't* have to ask.

'*Meu Deus*! I took forever. I felt humiliated and angry even thinking about it. I wanted to stay angry at everyone – it seemed easier to be mad than swallow my considerable pride and ask a favour. I was also frightened that they would say no. I finally telephoned my mother and asked her if she would babysit one evening so Amelia and I could go out for dinner. She burst into tears. She said she thought we didn't trust her and Papa to take care of Alberto because we had never asked her to help.

'What a lesson this taught me. I've apologised to my brother and sister, which I think was even harder than asking my mother to take care of my son.'

It is easy to spend time telling ourselves why we can't do something rather than trying it and finding out. You may not be surprised the way Silvio was and have a great outcome. In his case, both 'sides' were completely wrong in their thinking – they all had hamster-wheel thoughts that could have escalated even more if Silvio hadn't been willing to try something new. I hadn't asked Silvio to resolve anything, to try to make it all right for others, to get to the bottom of anything. We just focused on one rule he could try to break and see what the consequences would be. The consequences could just have easily been that his mother wasn't interested, she had done enough child caring in her life, she didn't want any more responsibility. He didn't know until he tried.

Repetition alert

Although this book is clearly focused on family dynamics, as I'm on the topic of patterns, I thought it might be a good idea to point out that there is a very high likelihood that you may have some calcified thinking when it comes to other types of relationships, such as work colleagues, friendships or even casual acquaintances. You could very well find yourself repeating the same patterns and rules in this aspect of your life as you have with your families. It's very hard not to replicate what has happened in one part of our lives right smack in another.

For instance, I look back with cringing embarrassment at the fact that I had a couple of very good friendships that I cut off without a word when I was much younger. I did the silent treatment thing and didn't attempt to resolve our differences or clear the air or anything remotely ameliorating. When I was young, I just didn't have the insight to find a way through my feelings of hurt and betrayal, so I cut them out of my life just as my stepmother had cut her siblings out of hers and mine have cut me out of theirs. It took a long time for me to even realise that I was following a pattern of behaviour I had been taught since childhood.

Exercise six

Spend some time thinking about some of the other major relationships in your life. Notice if you have duplicated any rules, expectations, wishes and patterns in any of these relationships as you have in your family.

You might try breaking a rule or two or three in these relationships as well.

Repetition alert number two

This alert is for those of you out there with children. As rules and patterns are usually instilled in you when you are very young, you don't have much chance to question them till you're older – if you ever do. Therefore, they stay entrenched in your belief systems and, as I pointed out earlier, they feel like they are you – just the way you are. If this is so, there is a very real chance that you will pass these rules, patterns and beliefs onto your own children without even being aware of it. They will learn from your behaviour how they are supposed to act. They will pick up the unspoken rules and teach themselves how they are expected to conduct themselves without being told.

Exercise seven

Take some time to look at your own children's behaviour. Can you identify any patterns or rules that you have passed on to them? See if you can identify which rules or patterns you believe are helpful to them and which perpetuate some of the unhealthy dynamics in your family.

Work on patterns, rules and beliefs is a lifelong enterprise. Just when you think you've got a handle on one, another one comes and bites you on the bum. They may occasionally pat you on the head. I like quite a few of my patterns and beliefs – they sustain me and make me feel good about myself in the world. It's only when I become aware that some of the things I do are unhelpful, usually unconscious, and serve to reinforce some of my least attractive behaviour that I become uncomfortable and know I have to do something about them.

Things to be aware of:

Be aware of the ways in which you can get 'got' and who can 'get' you.

Be aware of any teasing techniques you use and what their impact is.

Be aware of the rules – spoken and unspoken – patterns and beliefs you and other members of your family follow.

Be aware of any rules, etc that have been passed down through the generations, including any you might be passing on to your children.

Be aware of any resistance you have to breaking your family rules and patterns.

Be aware of any replicating you are doing in other areas of your life outside the family.

Be aware of how much chat you may have going on in your head when you think about changing your behaviour.

Things you could try:

Try breaking a rule or changing a pattern at your next family get-together.

Once you've broken one, break another. And then another.

As you gain more practice, go back to Chapter Four and pick out another role you play and change it.

6

Deposits and Withdrawals from the Memory Bank

Ancient history

Funny how our brains are like computers, with everything bad that ever happened to us indelibly recorded in our internal microchips. We can remember our mother's raised eyebrow from four decades ago, even if we can't remember what our partner said two minutes ago. Of course, we may very well remember the good times, but I've noticed that it's the unpleasant, humiliating and shameful incidents that are far easier to recall than the happier or more pleasant memories. It's these memories that can also stop us from dealing with our families more effectively especially at family get-togethers.

At family events, we don't just live in the moment and experience what's going on right then and there, a lot us have the tendency to experience our families through the filter of what happened previously. In other words, you can be at your grandparents' golden wedding anniversary and notice your siblings giggling in a corner. Instead of just noticing that they're giggling, you might withdraw a dusty and ancient memory of when they were giggling about some idiotic thing you had done that got you into trouble. You replay your embarrassment and shame; you recall in great detail how angry and resentful you felt towards them. Then one ancient memory leads to another one and you withdraw the next one from the memory bank as well and relive the feelings that caused you. You're on a roll now, and the memories come thick and fast as you summon up all those yucky feelings you endured at their hands. It no longer matters what they might actually be giggling about now, it's the memories that take over and the emotions you experienced in the past.

It could be that whoever it is you have strong feelings about doesn't even have to do anything to trigger your memories. They just have to exist. You may have an Axis of Evil or two just as Fred does. The person just has to exist to set off your computer search of past misdemeanours, slights, unhappy encounters, etc.

I think of parts of my family as being Champion Grudge Holders. That's where the strength of will comes from to be able to resist talking to your nearest and clearly not dearest for decades. Holding a grudge because of something that was done to you forty years ago is really something.

Maintaining a grudge usually means you have to top it up though with more proof that you were right all along and what was done to you was truly awful. Your memory bank is probably also greedy for deposits of new snubs, insults and grievances that you can store away for future use. Remember that proof-finding I mentioned in Chapter Two, where you look for proof that your worst misgivings are true? All those proofs get deposited in the memory bank no matter how valid, true or false they are.

All these memories gain interest as well – far more than any real bank. You compound the memories with new twists and variations and get very bloated accounts.

I may be making light of all this and I don't mean to minimise the impact that past events have had on you. I certainly know that many things that happened in my life, especially when I was younger, blighted my experiences and made family gatherings torturous at times, and undoubtedly those things can affect present gatherings as well. However, what I am aware of in myself and in others is that the memories can take precedence and I can't see clearly what's right in front of me. I experience current situations through the filter of my unhappy past and that isn't always the wisest and certainly not the healthiest thing to do.

My light-hearted approach is poking a little fun at my own immature behaviour and at yours as well. If we can laugh about it, admit we're 'guilty' and be aware of what we do, then we have a chance of changing this aspect of our family dynamics as well.

Spreading the word

Given the chance, we'll withdraw those memories and plonk them in front of anyone who will listen and replay all the old songs about how hard done we were way back when. But take a look at who we plonk our stories in front of: family members who we believe are in our 'camp', friends, even sympathetic-looking recent acquaintances will all hear our stories. We can be kind of indiscriminate when we start spreading the word of just how awful our cousin was, our mother, our brother-in-law, our son. Many of us seem to lose our sense of discretion when we start talking about our families and family get-togethers. What this pattern of behaviour tends to do is to reinforce the beliefs we have about the hellish members of our family.

Rarely does anyone repeat their stories with the aim of gaining insight and resolution. Stories are told to elicit sympathy, to reinforce strong emotions, to gain allies, to validate the memory and make it real. Sometimes stories are told just as a way of letting off steam. Nothing wrong with any of that except all it does is keep the family dynamics as stuck as they always have been. I know that when I used to tell my stories it helped me perpetuate unhealthy family dynamics; I tended to nurse them, eventually embellishing them so that the stories became more black and white as time went by. It's only as I've grown older that shades of grey have entered my perceptions; maybe it wasn't quite as I remembered it after all. I'm not diminishing the impact of what happened to me, but I have developed the ability to see situations through more than just my eyes.

This doesn't mean that I still don't occasionally make juicy withdrawals and present my accounts – ta-da! – so that someone new gets to hear my sorry tales. Sometimes I'm able to recount my memories through my mature eyes, and sometimes I find it quite difficult to maintain any distance at all and I can't or won't see them through anything other than my own hurt eyes.

Not only that, we rarely sit down with the 'villains of the piece' and talk with them about our memories, our stories. Everyone else hears about how awful our uncle or our sister-in-law or our daughter or father is. Everyone else hears about what 'they' have done and how awful it is. Too often, the only time we tell the other family member how we feel is in a circular argument, shouting match or accusation where we throw around those popcorn statements and never really get to the heart of the matter.

Our stories, our withdrawals, seem to exist to keep our family relationships stuck rather than moving forward.

Which is where we're going in a minute. But first I want to talk about the nature of memory.

Remembrance of things past

Did Marcel Proust know just what he was doing when he wrote about chomping into a madeleine?

Sense memories happen to all of us. A smell, a taste, a sound, a touch, a sight will transport us delightedly or miserably back to a distant time and place. There's a certain earthy smell I only very occasionally get whiff of, but when I do I'm right back in the woods behind my father's house where I used to retreat to when things were too fraught at home. We all have countless ones and it's always interesting to experience a sense memory because they can take us by surprise. With many of our best memories we'll try to recreate them by having certain scents around and foods to eat. We'll have photos of some of our happier get-togethers to remind us of fun times, and just about all of us have music that will evoke good remembrances of times past.

When recalling unpleasant and unhappy memories there are generally feelings attached to them. Those feelings can often distort the very thing we are remembering. The brain is stupendously complex and scientists are still (and I imagine will be for a very long time) discovering new information about how the brain works. Part of the work scientists are doing is on memory: how we store it, how we retrieve it, how memories change just by the mere fact of our repeatedly storing and retrieving them.

Sometimes family memory can be a bit like the old Soviet Union: our histories get rewritten by whoever has the most power. This is the way it was and no arguing. Rewritten history can have quite a powerful bearing on things. In the face of someone's emphatic insistence on having the right facts at hand it's easy to start questioning your own memory. 'I don't think that's what happened,' can turn into 'Did it really happen like that?' which in turn can turn into, 'Maybe it did happen like that.'

Fred has very little memory of his early years, even into adolescence, so a lot of 'his' memories are stories he's been told about what his life was like, rather than what he can actually recall. This means that his early memories aren't his own; they're someone else's perception of what happened to him. As he's got older, some memories have come back, but whole chunks of his younger years have still been 'written' by other people.

Of course, history is more like varying 'eyewitness accounts': everyone has a different version of what actually happened. I talk to my older sister and wonder if we were actually in the same place at the same time – her view is so different from mine. Well, of course it is, we're different people. It just feels weird when families start to reminisce and you try to find your personal reality in other people's stories ('No, no it wasn't like that at all!').

Exercise one

Identify an incident from a recent family get-together that you were unhappy about. Write out what happened and what your feelings about it were. Name the main 'players' and what their roles were. Now ask as many people who were there what happened.

Challenge number one

Here's the first challenge. See if you can ask each person what happened without putting your own personal spin on it, without infusing your questions with your point of view. For instance, you could ask a sibling, 'I'd like to hear your point of view about last Sunday lunch at Mum and Dad's.' Or would you want to say instead, 'So what did you think about how rude Dad was to Mum last Sunday?'

Can you simply ask family members what happened without any additional spin?

Challenge number two

The second challenge is to see if you can listen to them without trying to convince them of your point of view. For instance, 'Oh come on, you don't really think Mum brought it on herself; Dad was impossible!'

If you find it difficult to ask others who were present what their point of view was, can you imagine how they might have seen the situation?

Having got a variety of points of view, now take a look to see if there are any differences in outlook. Did anyone see it differently? Were there alternative interpretations on what happened? How do you feel about them all? Do you feel triumphant if your sister's version is just like yours? 'I was right! Dad was awful to Mum.' Or frustrated and impatient when your brother didn't notice anything amiss: 'They seemed all right to me.' 'What do you mean all right? They could barely look at each. Don't you ever notice anything but yourself?'

This is an exercise I encourage you to repeat a few times just to have the experience of hearing different points of view. Of course, it may be that people will have seen and felt the same things you did, but it is unlikely that they'll be exactly the same.

But I wanna be right

Most people spend inordinate amounts of time justifying their own points of view without attempting to see someone else's. And then insisting that others agree with them at the same time. When I was younger I really, really had to be right. Being right felt like life or death and if I did get into an argument not only did I have to be right, but the other person had to be wrong. Being right makes people feel in some kind of control (spurious, of course, given the way family hell get-togethers tend to play themselves out) when they are under stress and in alien territory.

A spin-off of point-of-view justifying is the need to seek out allies (as in the above example) to prop up biased arguments. I was pretty good at this too, collecting people who would agree with me so that I felt better about myself. I'm beyond being embarrassed now, but I have to ask myself, 'Why did I need to be right?' I know I said it's about control, but I think it's a lot more than that. I believe our need to be right is about seeking validation, and I additionally believe that this need exists in just about everyone.

We want to be validated by the people we love and by the people we may not love but wish they loved us. When I was younger, I could hear the loveliest things said about me by friends and work colleagues, but without the validation from family, their words slid right off me – it was my family from whom I needed to hear lovely things.

Without that, I tried to find it in other ways, which takes us back to the need to be right. If I could get enough people on my 'side' then the battle was worth it. When I was battling to be right, I didn't take much time at all to see anyone else's point of view.

So the question for you is: when you are at a hellish family get-together, how much do you need to be right?

We'll return to this shortly.

How come they don't see what I see?

It's very hard to get enough distance from something you don't like to be able to see it really clearly. If your experiences are generally filtered through your emotions, it can feel impossible to accept that there are other interpretations. Much as it may be difficult to accept, other people will have utterly different, equally valid experiences of the same scenario. Hearing what other family members have to say could help you get some distance. More than that, however, is that when you can see things from other people's points of view, you can actually do some quite positive things to change the family dynamic.

Here's how.

To start with, I want to look at Tim, whose story I outlined in Chapters Three and Four. There was one particular family do that he felt typified what happens at his family get-togethers. I asked him to do the above exercise and this is the result.

First, the story.

Case study: Tim's story continued

'It happened this past Christmas. I really didn't want to spend Christmas Day at my parents' again. Every year, no matter what, we're all expected to show up right after breakfast to open presents and then sit through an interminable lunch, go for a long, usually damp and chilly walk and back for tea.

'I also had a girlfriend, Nella, I was getting serious about. You know, close to 40, time to settle down kind of thing. She wanted to go "home" to her parents and wanted me to come along. I didn't really want to do either; I just wanted the two of us to spend a quiet Christmas together without anyone else around.

'In the end we compromised and spent Christmas Eve with her parents, stayed overnight, had breakfast with them and got to my parents "late".

'Mum, as usual, criticised me as soon as we got there for not coming right after breakfast. Everyone had already opened their presents because they weren't going to let me spoil it for them. Dad said he was upset because I had upset Mum.

'My brother, David, of course, had probably been there since the crack of dawn so once again he was the golden boy who could do no wrong. He began to show off to Nella, talking about his great job, to show me up again because I was just a lowly teacher.

'After lunch, we all got ready to troop out but Mum said she was going to stay to do the washing-up. An almighty row flared up about our needing to be together, the washing-up could wait. As usual I got silent; Mum stayed behind looking exasperated; Nella put her arms through my dad and David's arms, chatting with them while I sulked a few steps behind.

'When we got back to the house, Mum had already set the table for tea, so everyone sat around pretending nothing had happened, and I made our excuses as soon as I put down my teacup.'

Months after this Christmas, I suggested to Tim that he ask everyone who was there how they experienced the day. No embellishments, no preambles, just a straightforward question: 'What do you remember about last Christmas?'

Here's what they said:

The answers Tim got

Nella: 'I thought you were a prat. You behaved like a little kid who didn't get his way. You didn't even really talk to anyone the whole day. I'd never seen you like that and I couldn't see what was wrong. Your mother was lovely to me and I enjoyed talking to your brother and father, even if you were trailing behind us – how pathetic. But I love you anyway.'

Mum: 'I was so glad to see you and Nella. I wished you'd got there earlier so you wouldn't miss out on opening the presents – I still like seeing my boys' faces when we get something just right for you both. The only cloud was when your father insisted I go out for a walk. I just wanted to get back in the kitchen to clear everything away and besides my feet hurt. I was sorry you and Nella left early.'

Dad: 'Christmas? That was ages ago. I don't know. Oh, yes, your mother refused to go out with us and I was pissed off about that, but Nella cheered me up. She's a good girl.'

David: 'I was relieved to see you – it's hard being there on my own without any backup. Weren't you upset about something? I thought maybe you and Nella had had a fight or something.'

Have you ever seen or heard of the Japanese film *Rashomon*? It's a film where a quite dramatic story is told from five different points of view. The film has become so synonymous with this practice that psychologists have a name for it: The *Rashomon* Effect. Many other films and books have used it – the US version of *Rashomon* was *The Outrage*, and recent films that have used the device include *Hoodwinked* and *Courage Under Fire*. Even an episode of *The Simpsons* had a reference to it.

The reason I bring it up is that to me, hearing other people's descriptions of the same event is like being plonked in the middle of a film where no two people have the same perception of what happened. Whose truth is the 'real' truth, and can there ever be such a thing?

In Tim's case, hearing what everyone had to say was a real eye-opener and not what he expected at all. He was chastened by what Nella had to say, but more importantly, he got a completely different view of his mother and brother.

Now, this is how I suggested he use that information at his next family get-together: 'Try to accept that your mother is happy to see you. It doesn't matter if she complains; see if you can ignore that part of her conversation and concentrate on making her feel as though you are happy to see her. David clearly feels you are more of an ally than you ever thought, so why don't you tell him something personal that's happening at work? See what happens. Given that you usually feel criticised for not visiting more often, rather than justifying why not, you could try to pre-empt their complaints by telling them you know how disappointed they are you don't stop by more often. This way you are acknowledging how they feel rather than focusing on how you feel. Apologise to Nella for being a prat.' These suggestions all came from the information he gathered and were made by helping him see things from their point of view.

I see where you're coming from

This is really key. I want to wave flags and sound bells here to get you to understand just how key this is and how you can use this very effectively at every difficult family gathering you have.

When you are able to put aside your own point of view, even for just a little while, and see something from someone else's, you have a fantastic opportunity to behave in new and improved ways. The idea of 'walking a mile in someone else's shoes' is all about being able to see even a tiny corner of the world from another perspective. It will be different from yours, no matter how similar you are in beliefs, temperament, ideologies, etc. When you are far apart in beliefs and temperament, it's even more important to be able to make the effort.

When you are able to do this, it's like you've been given secret (and magical) information which can help you in your family relationships. Heavenly families know how to do this big time. It doesn't matter if they do all the unhealthy things that hellish families do, their ability to see the same situation from multiple points of view gives them a considerable edge on resolving difficulties.

Here's what you can do with that magical information:

Exercise two

Take a piece of information you've gathered from hearing someone else's point of view. If you haven't got anything directly from the horse's mouth, then see if you can step into their shoes for a nanosecond and see the world, however briefly, the way they may be seeing it

Notice if any part of you wants to dispute it, contradict it, declare it wrong, wrong, wrong. Then imagine what you could say to them using their point of view as your starting point.

Here's another example that might help make it clear: I know someone who thinks her sister is pushy and always telling her how she should bring up her kids. My friend finds this impossible and now hates being around her sister because she knows she's going to get an earful. When we were chatting about it, I asked her if she could imagine what her sister's outlook might be. After a bit of resistance, she conceded that her sister probably thought she was doing it for her (my friend's) own good, trying to be helpful and hoping she wouldn't make too many mistakes bringing up her children. Therefore, I suggested that the next time she sees her sister about to open her mouth, she uses that assumption to pre-empt her saying anything. Possibly saying something such as, 'I know you really mean well, and I appreciate that you care. I probably am making lots of mistakes, but we seem to be muddling through OK.'

When other people's feelings and points of view are acknowledged they feel better about the person doing the acknowledging. It doesn't heal all wounds or make up for past hurts, but it does mean that you have taken a step towards them. We all like to feel appreciated and when you allow someone else their point of view instead of trying to convert them to your way of thinking, or feeling that they are utterly hopeless, you become more heavenly.

It also means that at some point you might be able to let go of a particular deposit in the memory bank.

This is an exercise that is used frequently in workshops my company runs because it is as valid in the business world as in the family one. If you can practise this one a lot, you will get very adept at seeing things from other people's perspective and you will become a far better, more effective communicator and relationship builder, no matter what those relationships are. It is a fabulous skill to have.

Ready for more?

Another step forward

Everything I have suggested and encouraged you to try out so far has been about you taking some action: thinking action or doing action. As promised in Chapter One, I haven't asked you to change your feelings, just what you do and think.

One common theme in family get-togethers that are stuck and just repeating old patterns is that it's quite easy to be passive. You may be someone who doesn't think you're passive or even look passive, especially if you're always in the middle of a fray or trying to sort things out. However, if nothing changes then the communication loop is going round and round instead of forward. That's what I mean by passive.

Another technique we use regularly on our workshops is called 'listening with empathy' and, once again, it's as effective for families as it is for business. This is about having a willingness to let the other person have their point of view and validating it. It's easier to give you an example first, which shows two different versions of the same disagreement.

Edward and Frank are brothers. Every year they go off to a resort in the Canaries with their wives, children and parents. This family holiday has been going on for years and years. This year Edward decided to introduce the idea of going somewhere new.

When I talked with Edward later, we discussed a possible alternative dialogue using the listening-with-empathy technique.

Version one is an example of circular arguing:

Edward: 'Shall we try some place new for the family holiday this year?'

Frank: 'What's wrong with going back to the Canaries? Everyone always likes it.'

Edward: 'But we've been doing the same thing for years now. I just thought it might be nice to try another city or even the countryside.'

Frank: 'We need something for the kids to do and we know what we'll get at the resort.'

Edward: 'Yes, but wouldn't it be fun to explore and have a different experience?'

Frank: 'Why do you always have to be different?'

Edward: 'I'm not being different, I just think we've been doing this too long.'

Frank: 'What's more important, the family, or you getting your own way?'

Edward: 'Of course the family is important, but as long as we're all together, then it doesn't matter where we are.'

Frank: 'Exactly. Which is why we should go back to the Canaries.'

This is an argument going nowhere fast.

Here's an alternative version using the listening-with-empathy technique. This technique requires you to really listen hard to what the other family member is saying and finding something in their argument to agree with. This does not mean giving up your point of view; it does not mean agreeing with everything they are saying. What you are looking to do is to take the fight out of the argument. What you are looking to do is validate their perspective instead of stomping all over it.

Here's what it might sound like using listening with empathy:

Edward: 'Shall we try some place new for the family holiday this year?'

Frank: 'What's wrong with going back to the Canaries? Everyone always likes it.'

Edward: 'You're right; everyone has enjoyed it every year.'

Frank: 'So what's the problem?'

Edward: 'No problem, I just thought the kids might like doing something a little different.'

Frank: 'We need something for the kids to do and we know what we'll get at the resort.'

Edward: 'That's true, the kids have had a good time in the past. They are getting older now.'

Frank: 'Well, I don't see why you're making such a fuss.'

Edward: 'It does seem as though I'm being difficult, doesn't it? I don't mean to be; I just thought somewhere new might be a good change.'

Frank: 'No, you're not being difficult, it just feels like a lot of work making different arrangements.'

I don't know how this argument might end or resolve itself. Eventually, Edward and Frank might even get to what's really going on. But I'm showing you there are ways of avoiding getting hooked into another pointless, frustrating and going-nowhere fight.

In each part of the exchange, Edward listened to what Frank was saying and used it to soften the disagreement. Edward didn't give in or change his point of view. What he changed was his approach. He was more flexible and less dogmatic so that he left more room for Frank to give a little.

In the first dialogue, both Edward and Frank jumped into the ring, gloves on and aiming to land as many punches as possible. In the second suggested dialogue, Edward lowered his fists and metaphorically stepped out of the ring. He chose not to engage with the fight, instead he focused on the issue no matter what his brother threw at him. Every time Frank threw another punch, he moved away and didn't attempt to punch his brother back. He listened, used what he heard and attempted to give his brother a different experience of himself. In addition, he didn't make Frank wrong or contradict him; he let him be right; he validated his point of view and he conceded that maybe he was being a bit of a pain.

Exercise three

You could try practising this with a good friend before you try it out at your next family do.

Go back to a hellish family get-together, find an argument or disagreement you had. Withdraw it from your memory bank and, if you are able, write out the dialogue as I did above. If you don't want to go to the trouble of writing it all out, if you're like me, you probably remember everyone's lines verbatim anyway. You don't need to have more than a few lines of the most difficult or frustrating part of the fight/heated discussion.

Using empathy, see if you can rewrite (or rethink) your lines to include something the other person said in a validating, acknowledging way.

If you practise this particular technique of listening with empathy and get proficient at it, you will be able to transform many of your disagreements and disputes without resorting to verbal violence or provoking it in someone else.

One word of caution . . . 'but. . .' This is a common mistake people make when using this technique – they slip in a little 'but'. For example, 'Yes, but. . .' or 'I agree with you, but. . .' or 'You have a good point, but. . .' Using 'but' is seductive. It's like having a foot in two camps. You'll try the empathy bit, but you're not going to appear a pushover. 'But' says, 'I'm right and you're wrong.'

It'll take practice; eventually, when you get really good at it, you'll find you won't be using the 'but'; you won't need to use the 'but'.

Strings or no strings?

When it comes to families, there are a hell of a lot of strings attached, aren't there?

There are 'good' strings, such as love and affection, compassion and nurturing. We are tied to those in our family, where we feel connected through the giving and receiving of genuine care. There are less good strings where we are tied to family members through old patterns, unhealthy communication loops, wishful thinking and our unrequited yearning for love, affection, compassion and nurturing.

Every time we deposit into or withdraw from our memory banks in anger, frustration or resentment the 'harmful' strings get tighter. We are bound to people for all the wrong reasons.

What if I introduce the word 'forgiveness' into the family equation? Interesting word, forgiveness. It's our ability to stop resenting someone's behaviour, what they've done to us. It's the ability to let go of grudges and past hurts. It's letting other family members have their points of view even if we don't agree with them.

How can forgiveness be a technique? My immediate thought is that it's kind of religious or spiritual: turn the other cheek, live and let live, do unto others as you would have them do unto you.

Morris felt the same way.

Case study: Morris's story continued

'Forgiveness? Isn't that kind of a religious thing? I'm not religious really; I go to synagogue on High Holy Days but that's about it. This smacks of being a goody-goody to me.

'The idea of forgiving my mother and sister really went against the grain. I wanted *them* to apologise so then *I* could forgive *them*. I wanted them to tell me they really they cared about me and were sorry they excluded me, that they were proud of me. I wanted them to realise they were this secret cabal they didn't let me into. Sure, I'd forgive them if they asked for my forgiveness, if they apologised, I could do that and be magnanimous.

'I really couldn't get my head around the whole idea of forgiving them. It was puzzling to me what you meant. You know, I thought I just wouldn't believe it – it would just be words I'd be thinking. I wouldn't really be feeling forgiving. "OK, I forgive you." What does that mean? I'd be pretending, making it up.

'Then I thought, well, what the hell am I forgiving them for? For not treating me well? For liking each other's company more than mine? For not loving me enough? This was getting too complicated and I didn't like it. So I stopped thinking about it and decided I wasn't going to do anything 'cause I still couldn't get my head round it at all.

'Then one day the light bulb went on. I realised that it wasn't about forgiving them, not at first it wasn't. It was – boy, does this sound corny – it was about forgiving myself. For what though? It seemed the right thing to do, but if I couldn't figure out what I'd be forgiving them for, I wasn't sure what I'd have to forgive in myself.

'I did finally figure it out. I think I'm a slow learner here. I forgave myself for all my unkind thoughts, my disappointments and my expectations that they should treat me differently. All those resentments I kept bottled up weren't getting me anywhere. I was spending a lot of time thinking all these negative thoughts. I was getting ready to retire from my job and yet I still felt small. I felt ashamed for wanting their love.

'When I began to forgive myself, something changed inside and I could look at them differently.'

Life isn't always like Morris's. He had to work exceptionally hard to get to the place where he could forgive.

Forgiveness means your memory bank account will shrink. Of course, you'll still have memories, but they aren't taken out and used as a weapon or as currency to keep resentments going, old hurts present in your mind and wounds continually filled with fresh salt.

Forgiveness, as Morris rightly pointed out, isn't something you just say. It does have to be genuine. And in Morris's case he never actually said anything to his mother and sister directly. The forgiveness was internal, but afterwards his feelings towards them did change enough so that he could enjoy being with them in ways he hadn't before. His sister didn't miraculously become his best friend, he didn't have a weeping reconciliation with his mother; it was simply easier to be with them and his thoughts were quieter.

The heavenly families I know have a remarkable gift for forgiveness. Like all of us, they get hurt, upset, frustrated, enraged. Other family members can get up their noses and do things that are thoughtless and inconsiderate. Yet, they don't have bloated memory banks where they are depositing yet more proof of just how bad the other person is.

So how does the idea of forgiveness sit with you?

Exercise four

Remind yourself of another family get-together from the hellish end of the spectrum.

Again, identify who did what that made it hellish. Who were the worst 'culprits'?

Is what they did forgivable?

Who	What they did	Forgivable?

There's no question that there are times when the things your family members do may very well be unforgivable. I certainly know that, though I'm much better at this forgiveness thing, there is still someone in my family, long dead, who I have not yet been able to forgive. Will I ever? I don't know. I'm still working on it. Thinking it doesn't make it genuine . . . not yet it doesn't. However, if you do have extremely strong feelings about someone who has behaved in an 'unforgivable' way and you still have them in your life, there has to be a question about how healthy that can be for you.

I will talk further about walking away in Chapter Eight, but for now it is useful to flag up that there are some situations that are genuinely unresolvable, and that for your own well-being, you have to ask yourself that if you cannot forgive, why do you still have a relationship with this person or people? Even if you can forgive and yet the situation is still unresolvable, staying in it will continue to undermine your own sense of self.

Fred and I forgave his parents for their alcoholism; we felt they were unhappy and vulnerable and suffered in their own lives. Yet, we knew that for our own health we could not continue going to family get-togethers because they never changed, they never got better and they were, at the time, a continual replay of repeated and very old pain.

So I am certainly not saying that there is anything wrong with the inability to forgive. However, in my experience talking to hundreds of people over the years, often the stuff we can't forgive has a great deal to do with the circular chat going on in our heads and less to do with what actually happened.

What about you? Do you find your insides bridling at the thought of forgiving people in your family for their impossible behaviour? Are you someone who says, 'OK, I can forgive, but I certainly can't forget'? Got to keep those bank balances high.

This is hard for many people. It's hard to give up grudges

you've been used to carrying around; it's hard to give up feeling hard done by and hard to give up wanting them to make the first move.

What are you holding on to and why are you holding on to it?

What I'm holding on to	**Why I'm holding on to it**

Perhaps I've done this the wrong way round, but now I'd like you to look at yourself, at the things you may need to forgive yourself for.

One of the things that helped me feel better about my sister was that I forgave myself for feeling so jealous of her. What I realised was that whether it was true or not that my parents loved her more than they loved me, it wasn't her fault. She wasn't responsible for how they felt about her or me, and she certainly wasn't responsible for how I felt about her. That was a turning point, forgiving myself for giving her a hard time, especially in my head – oh the thoughts I churned round and round!

What do you need to forgive yourself for?	**Can you do it?**	**If not, why not?**

Forgiveness isn't one of those techniques you learn as far as I'm concerned; it's something that gradually comes out of deeper understanding and awareness and, most importantly, feeling better about yourself. My hope is that as you learn to cope better at family get-togethers, you will indeed start feeling better about yourself. Forgiveness is something to return to again and again. Forgiveness takes maturity which is where we're going in the next chapter.

Things to be aware of:

Be aware of how many grudges you may still be harbouring.

Be aware of to whom and how often you tell you your stories.

Be aware that everyone sees things from a different point of view than yours.

Be aware if you are trying to collect allies that agree with your point of view.

Things you can try:

Try asking everyone who was an 'eyewitness' to a particular family difficulty what they saw. See if you can do this from a neutral position, without trying to convince them of your point of view or question theirs.

Try talking to one or two of your difficult family members by incorporating their point of view in your conversation; this is to make them feel validated and acknowledged.

Try listening with empathy, which will also make them feel heard; avoid using the word 'but' while trying out this technique.

Try emptying out your bank account, even just a little.

Try forgiving yourself.

Try forgiving some of your family members.

7

You're Not 12 Any More

When we were very young

I've been looking forward to this chapter ever since I started writing this book. This is the chapter where it's time to grow up.

Most of us are stuck in arrested development. We're stuck somewhere in time at 4 or 6 or 15, and given the right environment ('Oh Mum'), we'll revert to that age in a split second no matter what our proper age is right now. You might be 55, but have your father look at you with 'that look' and you start defending yourself the same way you did at 18.

Well, clearly it's only arrested development at certain times and with certain people. Our families, for the most part. This is all linked to our vulnerability in being able to get 'got'; to be wrong-footed, embarrassed, hurt or frustrated by members of our own family. When that happens we lose our adult identity almost instantly and revert to feelings and behaviours we had when we were little and felt powerless. Somehow, all over again, we can feel feeble in the face of the family dynamic.

Family get-togethers, of course, replicate so much of our young lives. Even with new people added to the mix (partners, stepmothers/fathers, in-laws, etc), it's reasonable to assume the family dynamics will be much as they have always been.

There you are at some event – a birthday party, picnic, christening – and, like a time traveller, someone just has to say something or do something that gets under your skin and you're right back in the past and feeling as inconsequential as you did then. You lose the power as adults in these situations. You're probably waiting for other family members to treat you differently, and when those family members don't, you relapse and become victims yet again to past family dynamics being played out over and over in the present. If, in the midst of a family get-together, someone acts as they always have, the power dynamic in the family stays exactly the same.

I don't want to go too deeply into the far past of your life, but I do know that when we're young, we are fairly, if not completely defenceless; the adults around us hold all the cards. They can either acknowledge that even though little, we are individuals in our own right or they can play out their own insecurities and we get caught in the crossfire.

A very simple model to illustrate this is that healthy families want to bolster their children's self-confidence and sense of security. In less than healthy families all the uncertainty, anxiety and fear that the adults might be feeling are passed on to the children. Usually, the adults are too caught up in their own problems and complications so that it's hard for them to really see what their children need to become whole people.

As I say, this is a very simplistic model and all families have shades of grey – hellish families have heavenly times and heavenly families have hellish times. It is the ability to see and understand what's going on as it's going on that distinguishes the two.

I can look back with great compassion now to growing up with my father and stepmother. I have a far greater understanding of the emotional difficulties my stepmother was experiencing and her own insecurities than I could possibly have had then. I have a far greater appreciation of my father and his disappointments and pressures than I could ever have imagined when I was young. I remember painful Thanksgiving meals, uneasy Sunday lunches and excruciating birthday parties where there was sure to be some argument, angry outburst or tearful accusation. All of us were on tenterhooks, hoping we'd get through the event without one, but that anxiety was always there.

It hasn't changed. The last family get-together we siblings had, I still felt on tenterhooks, I was still anxious in case something happened and, as described in Chapter Five, it did. The anxiety I felt when I was a child I still carried with me into adulthood, and I expect the same is true for most of you reading this. The feelings we experienced at hellish family get-togethers then, will still be sloshing around in us now.

When we were very young most of us had no say in the matter, no rational discussion to take part in, no guidance to explain what was going on. If the grown-ups around us were operating out of their own immature reactions to life, what chance did we have?

Now that we're grown-ups ourselves we don't expect to feel the same sense of powerlessness we did then and are disappointed and angry when we do. I certainly am. 'Hey, I'm a grown-up here! You can't talk to me like that.' Hmmm. All the while we behave like a 12 year old, we'll be treated as such.

I'll explain a little more. If, when you were young, you felt helpless in the face of the adult behaviour around you, the chances are that that's one of the patterns you will take right into your adulthood. You won't necessarily be conscious that that's what's happened, but as discussed earlier, patterns aren't usually conscious. A dynamic was created between you and the other members of your family that probably exists to this day: it is unlikely your feelings will have matured as your body has. Therefore, when something unpleasant or difficult happens at a family get-together, it's inevitable that you will react as you did in the past. Everybody around you will be doing the same thing. When you do that you are duplicating – and reinforcing – the old, unhealthy dynamic. You won't be reacting as your mature, adult self, you'll be reacting as you did then.

Case study: Li's story continued

'I'm a well-respected doctor at a very busy hospital. I studied for years to achieve my goal. I have two wonderful children and a good marriage – a successful and busy life. My patients rely on me, my children and husband rely on me and I like being relied on.

'When I'm with my parents, I seem to be caught in this in-between place. I feel I must respect their sense of tradition, honour our ancestors and take part in many holidays and celebrations which don't mean the same thing to me and my family. On the other hand, they haven't fully integrated into life in Bonn even after all these years (especially my mother), so I have to take care of them as though they were children, organising their paperwork and translating legal documents and such.

'My problem is that when I'm with them, even doing all the things they need, I feel like a 15 year old who's going to be told off for not studying hard enough, for spending too much time with foreign friends ("I'm the foreign one, Ma!"), for not taking the Mid-Autumn Festival seriously.

'If they start criticising me, I hear myself using the same whiny voice I did then trying to explain myself. In thinking about it now, I realise that probably anywhere else in the world parents would be proud if one of their children wanted to become a doctor, which is what I had decided when I was 15. Not mine. They were disappointed I wasn't studying to become a traditional Chinese doctor and no matter how successful I am, I feel the heavy burden of their disappointment and I know I feel as angry and frustrated as I did 20 years ago.'

Li is a good example of someone who reverts to her childish anxiety when she's with her family. She makes herself miserable and that must have an impact on the people around her. She's responding with the same sense of responsibility and guilt she had as a younger person.

Each of us tends to have an age where things really got stuck. Mine was 12, not surprisingly. Although life had some really grim moments up to then, a whole lot of stuff happened in my family (and to me specifically) when I was 12 and I know that overall that's when the emotional development of my family relationships stalled. Which is why, when my stepmother died and I was with all my siblings, I didn't feel particularly adult and things happened that the adult in me would have handled very differently. That adult me wasn't so present at the time. Nor in my siblings either.

What I do know is that unless we have a mature and strong healthy way of behaving when we are with our families, all of us will lapse into immature (dare I say, infantile) behaviour when we're under stress. And there's nothing like a hellish family get-together to create a little stress in our lives.

Exercise one

If you are able, try to put a specific age to your arrested development; to the age you revert to when the family get-together is at its worst.

It might help to think of some of the roles you identified in Chapter Four and see if you can remember how old you were when you started playing any of them. I can remember exactly when I became a Rebel with a Cause (12 years old, of course); it was brewing for a while, but this period was my first public manifestation of the role I'm still playing out today.

The age I revert to under stress is ______________

Can you remember what might have been going on in your life at the time? I did say this book isn't intended to do too much delving, however, personally, I have found it helpful to place myself back in time so that I can haul that 12-year-old self closer to the proper age I am now.

What was going on in my life back then?

____

____

____

____

____

____

Can you remember when you started adopting any of your roles and why?

Role	When and why I adopted it

Let's pretend

Along with the many roles we take on as children and carry into adulthood, we also learn to pretend. Now, of course, all children, everywhere, learn to pretend; it's how we stretch our imaginations and create magical worlds in which to retreat. We like to imagine we're the beautiful princess trapped in a tower, the baseball hero who hits the crucial home run at the World Series or the street urchin who saves a wealthy man's life and is rewarded with great riches. Pretending is fun.

There's another kind of pretending that isn't so much fun and serves to further bolster our roles, undermine our self-esteem and limit the way we are viewed by our relatives. This is the kind of pretending where we learn to hide our real selves and present an artificial self to a great part of the world.

Case study: Nisar's story continued

'I've been pretending to my family ever since I realised I was gay. You can't be gay and be a good Muslim; it's considered as corrupt as adultery. Every once in a while I think I'm going to say something to my family, tell them about me and Kasim.

'Then I'd have a terrible choice. I could repent and be forgiven and promise never to be with Kasim or any gay man again. I could say I won't/can't repent and then I will be ostracised by my family and my community.

'I keep pretending and somehow hope that after a while, everyone else will pretend as well and stop trying to marry me off. As long as I don't say anything, then maybe Kasim and I will be sort of accepted but not acknowledged as a couple.

'I've thought of leaving Pakistan and moving back to Britain, but then I would be just as cut off from my family who I love.'

This is why we can so often feel as though we are in the alien territory I described in Chapter Three. We feel alien because we are pretending.

In Nisar's case, he may never be able to resolve this terrible dilemma. It may be that he will eventually have to walk away from his family in order to be true to himself and his relationship. Pretending takes a serious toll.

It certainly did with me. I was the 'good girl' in my family. I had to pretend to be this good girl, no matter what was going on around me and no matter what I was feeling. In order to have a safety valve, I became the Rebel with a Cause, because, among the many reasons I chose this role, I could be less good if I was marching for nuclear disarmament or plunging myself into the civil rights movement. Because I believed I always had to show this good-girl front, I couldn't really be disobedient and I did just about anything I could to avoid getting yelled at or smacked. I somehow justified to myself that trying to get my sister in trouble wasn't being naughty (amazing what the mind can do, isn't it?). The more I had to keep up the front, the more I got used to pretending.

You will have pretended, too. You will have presented one person to your family, while another one existed right alongside, as though in a parallel universe. In my mind this is one of the main reasons why the family get-together can be so difficult – we're still pretending.

I am *not* a 'good' girl. Oh no. I'm outspoken, I speak my mind, I can be a real troublemaker. My main aim in life is not about pleasing people. It used to be because that was part of the invented me. Now, I'm not saying there's anything wrong with trying to please people – it's a lovely thing to do. However, like the roles I assumed, my pretending was running me, I wasn't running it. It was as knee-jerk as being the Human Buffer. It got lugged into my adult life as effectively as the roles and has certainly been a challenge to give up.

Another significant downside to pretending is that all the while you know you are doing it (and you *do* know), you don't feel so good about yourself. Who are you really when you're with your family? When you dutifully go to a cousin's wedding or spend time with a whole gang of in-laws and you find yourself smiling till your face hurts or laughing too loud at someone's unfunny jokes, are you being polite or are you working hard to keep up a pretence that you are someone you're not? Heavy stuff.

This is another stuck-behaviour loop: you pretend to be someone you're not so you don't feel particularly good about yourself. You don't feel so good about yourself and then your self-esteem and self-confidence takes a plunge. Your self-esteem gets lower so you don't have the confidence to try out new behaviour so you keep on pretending.

Let's pretend – part II

Here are a few family examples of pretending: let's pretend that everything's all right; let's pretend there's nothing wrong in the family; let's pretend we all get along; let's pretend that someone's utterly inexplicable, inappropriate and out-of-line behaviour is all right.

Families have an astonishing capacity to keep up such pretences for decades, lifetimes, generations. This pretending, however, creates a level of inherent dishonesty within the family, which will display itself in strange and unpleasant ways during family get-togethers.

Many, many years ago Fred and I went to friend's family New Year's Eve bash. We hadn't exactly been looking forward to it, but we liked the friend and so went along to support him with his seemingly normal family. The food was yummy and things were going relatively all right. Around 11.00 pm the host disappeared, just took himself off to his bedroom without a word to anyone. No 'I'm not feeling too well, I hope you'll excuse me.' No 'Sorry to be a party-pooper, but I just have to lie down.' No nothing. After a while it seemed even stranger that it was getting close to the midnight hour and still no sign of the host. The hostess was doing that 'everything's just hunky-dory' forced-smile thing; midnight came and went and we all went home gossiping about the missing host. Later, my friend told me that the hostess, her cousin, said to her that she hoped everyone had had a good time and that no one noticed hubby had absented himself. Hope no one noticed? Talk about cloud cuckooland. It turned out this was normal behaviour on his part, which no one in the family ever talked about, confronted him about, mentioned it might be rude or asked him what troubled him when he was with other people. Nothing. Silence in the face of clearly some form of distressed behaviour.

Let's pretend it isn't happening and maybe it will go away.

Exercise two: alien territory revisited

Can you identify when you started to pretend in order to protect yourself within your family? What did you pretend? What was the made-up self you showed to your family?

How much are you still pretending today? What effect does that have on you?

Are there any other kinds of behaviour that people in your family pretend isn't happening? What impact does that have on everyone?

. . . I put away childish things

Roles serve a purpose when we're young, just as pretending did. They are created out of the material we had available to us at the time. They help us survive difficult times and, in whatever way possible, help us deal with stress that's quite a burden for a little person.

We may have chosen them in a manner of speaking, but we did so without conscious thought.

The problem is that we don't really need the roles or the pretending any more. However we've done it, we're all grown up now. However helpful those roles were, it's time to choose some new ones; it is time to put away childish things. The problem with this is that we're used to the behaviour we exhibit when we're with our families and they're used to it as well. It's hard to give things up, so I'm not going to suggest you do that.

In Chapter Four, I suggested you try a new role and, in Chapter Five, I suggested you break a rule or pattern. I suggest working this way because in my experience it is easier to *do* something than it is to *stop* doing something. When you go about making changes from this approach, there's less danger of feeling a failure because you weren't able to stop doing the thing you set out to stop doing. Although in Chapter Four I encouraged you to choose a different role or two, just about all the roles on that list have a childish element to them because they were taken on when we were children. As I have said, there is nothing intrinsically good or bad in roles, rules, patterns or even pretending, as long as they don't keep us stuck.

If you can project forward to the next family get-together coming up and your heart sinks to your toes, then a part of you is still well and truly stuck. Very much time to choose another way.

Childish vs childlike

Before I get on to alternative roles and behaviour, I want to make a distinction between childish and childlike. I do this because when I've worked with people in the past many have said to me something along the lines of, 'But I like the little kid in me, why should I stop being childish?' Childish behaviour in an adult includes sulking, uncontrolled rages (even escalating into violence), demanding your own way, always expecting to be the centre of attention, being a sore loser, spending time in magical thinking (if I wish it, it will be so) and much more I'm sure you can recognise.

They're the kinds of things we as children do before we learn there are more effective ways to communicate and relate to others. If we don't learn them, those behaviours remain unmodified and come out in totally inappropriate ways as adults.

Childlike behaviour, on the other hand, is joyful and enquiring; it's laughter, curiosity and delight. Being childlike is all the wonderful things about being a child: relishing the new, being creative and playful. Sadly, these are the behaviours that often get lost as we grow up, but they are the qualities we don't want to lose and shouldn't have to give up as adults. The less we pretend the more we are able to access our childlike self.

Exercise three

Conjure up a recent get-together and identify any childish behaviour you may have displayed.

My childish behaviour:

____

____

____

Now identify any childlike behaviour you may have displayed.

My childlike behaviour:

____

____

____

Can you remember the impact any of those behaviours had on any of your family?

The impact:

____

____

____

Case study: Christine's story continued

'I've grudgingly agreed that there are some good points about my brother-in-law. It's made it a little easier being around him, but the rest of us still seem to have a right go at each other whenever we get together.

'Last time was at my cousin's graduation party. There was Geoff all over my cousin, congratulating him before any of his *real* relatives could get to him. Without even thinking, I said to no one in particular, "Typical! It would be Geoff who has to be right in the centre of everything."

'Lisa was furious with me and told me to mind my own business. If Geoff wanted to tell Howard congratulations what did that have to do with us? Why was I being so snotty?

'Mum jumped in, trying to explain to Lisa why I was upset and at the same time kind of agreeing with Lisa that it didn't matter if Geoff got to Howard first. Lisa rounded on Mum, saying she didn't need to defend Geoff, he was perfectly capable of taking care of himself, thank you very much.

'I had a go at Mum, too; couldn't she see Geoff was just trying to show us all up? It was getting worse than a playground fight with a gang of five year olds.'

Horrible, funny. Except that for Christine and her family it wasn't funny at all. This is a good example of childish behaviour running rampant among a bunch of adults.

Adult behaviour

Uh-oh. Sounds kind of serious, doesn't it?

Becoming more adult is a serious business, especially around our families. It means being far more conscious than most people who are stuck in childish behaviour are able to be at the moment. Being more conscious (when you are with your families and your knees are being jerked and your goat is getting got) means you have to *actively* choose new behaviour. It requires conscious thought (or, as the Buddhists say, mindfulness) and I will not underestimate the effort that conscious thought takes.

Years ago, I was working with a couple who were just about as hellish as you could get. They appeared to have a willingness to try to work things out, which is why they were in couples' counselling, but their resistance was extreme. At one point, when I was describing the kind of new behaviours they needed to start practising, the wife snarled at me (yes, she actually snarled), 'But that means I have to think about everything I say.'

Yup. That's exactly what it means. Now, I don't think most of us can be that conscious all the time and think about everything we say at all times. However, as you practise adult behaviour with your family, you may have to do a lot more looking before you leap to start with.

Here are some adult behaviours and roles to look at, to think about and then to start choosing:

Have an overview

This is the ability to see what's going on for all parties involved. It's having a bird's-eye view and being able to see the family dynamics, the roles people are playing and the rules they are following. When you are able to see clearly, you can then carefully explain to others what you see happening around all of you.

Separate yourself from the situation

To help with the previous behaviour, separating yourself from the situation helps you get an overview.

Tough. This one is tough. You are in the situation, so how on earth can you separate yourself from it? I know I've found myself in the maelstrom of a family hoo-ha and at the same time been able to be outside it looking in. The real skill is to be able to be separate without being detached; to understand the emotions going on without feeding them; to create breathing space where you might be able to see new options.

See other people's point of view

This was described in great detail in the previous chapter and also requires some distance from the fray to look at one situation from different perspectives. Once you have done that, you can introduce those differing perspectives in order to help others feel as though their outlook is just as valid as anyone else's.

I also call this showing understanding because you demonstrate that you do grasp what other people are trying to get across and perhaps by articulating what you understand you help others get their message across.

Acknowledge

I've noticed how hard it is sometimes to tell family members we don't get on with very well nice things about them. Like Christine, who was reluctant to find anything positive in her brother-in-law, a lot of people focus on the negative. Truly adult behaviour is the ability to cut through the haze of negativity and notice positive qualities, but more than that, it is the ability to tell the other person those positive qualities that have been identified. Christine would have to take the next bold step of telling Geoff that she appreciates how well he takes care of Lisa.

Encourage

Here you have to see what your family members are good at and encourage them to do more of it. If you have a son whose passion is for music you can't relate to, it can be very easy to poke fun at this passion or criticise it or feel fed up with the music he's always playing. As an adult, you can still encourage his interest and support his passion instead of disapproving of it.

Likewise, if your father starts mumbling about a new career, avoid telling him all the reasons why it would be unwise at his age, can he afford to retrain, isn't he putting the family at risk, blah, blah, blah. You could be excited for him, praise his courage and ask if there's anything you could do to help.

Listen with empathy

This is another behaviour from the previous chapter, where you listen carefully to what the other person is saying and put aside your own need to convince them that your view is the right one.

Then you listen to what they are saying till you find something to agree with (remember, you don't have to completely relinquish your point of view). You are looking to soften arguments, not escalate them.

Ignore the bait (look before you leap)

Now that you have spent time identifying your knee-jerk reactions and how you can get 'got', it is time to start practising ignoring the bait. This may mean biting your tongue – literally; it could mean calmly getting up and moving away from the bait-thrower or deflecting as in the empathy exercise above.

Ignoring the bait doesn't mean it doesn't affect you. I like to have inner chats with myself, along the lines of, 'Wow, that hurt. OK, I'm not going to say anything right now. I'll just wait it out.'

This is one of the most adult of all adult behaviours as far as I'm concerned because it requires all sorts of skills: understanding yourself more; then stopping your automatic behaviour; then not wanting to retaliate; and then, after all that, having ignored the bait, you're probably going to have to do something else completely different because the usual dynamic won't exist any more.

Stay calm in a crisis

In the midst of the *Sturm und Drang* of family get-togethers, it can feel impossible to be anything but calm. It's very easy to get caught up in the dramas others act out. Even if you do not feel it inside, staying composed may very well have a calming effect on others, especially if you're used to always throwing yourself into the middle of the vortex.

Avoid popcorn statements

This goes hand in hand with ignoring the bait. It requires you to really listen to what's coming out of your mouth ('But that means I have to think about everything I say!'), and making sure it's an appropriate response where you are attempting to shift the unhelpful status quo, not stay stalled in circular arguments.

Distinguish between diplomacy and tap dancing

You probably know what I mean by tap dancing: skirting the issues; not getting to the point; using lots and lots of words but never quite saying what's really on your mind. This is a 'clever' way of avoiding the issues.

On the other hand, sometimes you do need to be diplomatic. There's no point deliberately hurting someone when a kinder way is possible. However, it's easy to fall into the trap of avoiding the issues by convincing yourself you need to be diplomatic when you're frightened of dealing with something face on.

Put aside wishful thinking

I'm not sure we can ever completely give up some wisp of wishful thinking when it comes to close relationships; staying caught up in wishing things would change when in your heart you know they won't change is doing you harm. Facing this reality is another step to becoming more adult.

First, see if you can catch the moment when you hear yourself say, 'I wish my daughter/father/cousin/sister-in-law would ___________' (fill in the blank). Second, you can then say, 'Yes, I know I wish this, but it's not going to happen so it's best not to set myself up for disappointment, again.'

This is a start. It's to remind you that you do desire change, but it isn't necessarily going to come from them first. If you want change, it is you who has to make it happen.

Anticipate and forestall

At this point in your life, you pretty much know what's going to happen at one of your hellish family get-togethers. You have spent some time with this book identifying a lot of the unhealthy and inappropriate family dynamics, so you know what could happen the next time you gather with them.

Anticipating what might happen allows you to create a strategy. Instead of being a victim to events ('I know exactly what's going to happen; she's going to say the same old things and we'll end up in a row') you could plan your approach beforehand.

Let me explain a bit more. Even though you know exactly what's going to happen, or could happen, there's that glimmer of wishful thinking which hopes it will be different this time. So instead of planning a different strategy, you, like Charlie Brown, get taken in by your fantasies, and go to the next family event unprepared. Then you get 'got', even though you could have written the script ahead of time with all the words or deeds that create the disappointment, anger, frustration, etc.

If you start giving up wishful thinking it means you are seeing reality for what it is and then you can choose to do things differently.

See reality for what it is

This is similar to having an overview and seeing things from other people's points of view, but it's a lot more than that. In the putting aside of wishful/magical thinking and our fantasies that somehow it will all work out without our having to take any of the first steps, what's left is the stark reality of what is really going on in your family.

Fred used to say that when he thought about his parents they were always sober, understanding and responsive to their two children's needs. He knew this was Fantasyland but it was easier for him to cope with his hurt if he imagined them different from how they really were. It was only when he finally well and truly accepted that what he was seeing was two alcoholics, enmeshed in their own misery and unable to relate in an adult way with him that he knew he had to walk away.

Seeing reality for what it is doesn't mean you have to walk away, but it does mean you have to take the blinkers off and see what is right in front of you. You then have the option of deciding what is the best thing to do rather than reacting to your disappointments or making them wrong for not being how you wish them to be.

Show willingness; be flexible

I was really stubborn when I was younger – unmovable might be a better description. When I had an opinion or a course of action that I was determined about, not much could stay my hand. Willingness to see there was another way about just about anything was a challenge. It meant becoming a whole lot more flexible and genuinely wanting to see and initiate change. Willingness meant I had to enter the debate instead of being utterly sure of my position so, therefore, no debate was allowed.

Willingness means that you are open to hearing other people's opinions, wants and needs. Flexibility means making room for those opinions, wants and needs to happen even if they conflict with yours.

Try some lateral thinking

Old patterns and problems tend to create the same old solutions – that often don't work. It's easy to get so caught up in the pull of repeating the same old same old that we don't see that there's another – perhaps unusual – solution staring us in the face. Doing something different will change things, as I've said before. Having a go at something new will open more creative channels to keep looking for other new things to do or try out.

Allow, tolerate, accept

This seems suspiciously like forgiveness. It is.

Years ago I was given some advice by a wiser person than I that I didn't 'get' for quite a long while. It was, 'Let the other person be another person.' I resisted understanding this, let alone putting it into practice. The penny dropped eventually when I realised that I was trying to control the people in my life by wanting them to be clones of myself – I wanted them to think, feel and behave the way I did so I could feel better about myself. This comes under the same category as wanting to convince others that I'm right and they're wrong. In allowing people to be who they are, meant I'd have to put up with all sorts of things I didn't really approve of. So the understanding was all about knowing the difference between someone's behaviour that was detrimental to me as opposed to someone else's behaviour I just didn't like. This was hard. Like all these recommendations, it has got a lot easier over the years the more I do it.

Allowing requires you to distinguish between unhealthy behaviour and what gets up your nose. There are lots of things that people in my family do that get up my nose and I'm sure vice versa. So what? Who am I to be the arbiter of proper behaviour? Who am I to decide how others ought to conduct themselves?

Personality quirks or simply annoying behaviour?

Having said that, there's no reason why you can't let people know that some of the things they do you find annoying. Everyone has quirks and ways of behaving that are little niggly things which just get to you because they do. They aren't tied to any ancient history; they aren't connected to patterns and rules. They're just flat out annoying.

If you do decide to mention one of these annoying habits to someone remember to choose carefully.

Fred once told me he didn't like the way I slurped hot drinks. Instead of throwing the aforementioned hot drink in his face, I bargained with him and said I'd stop slurping in my annoying way if he stopped biting his nails loudly. Chomp, chomp and I wanted to throttle him. Slurp, slurp and he wanted to throttle me. It's worked pretty well so far. I pay attention to slurping and he pays attention to nail biting . . . when I remind him. I don't mind reminding him, because it's part of the bargain so I know I have a leg to stand on. And so much more effective than throttling him in the long term.

Being tolerant and allowing is a fabulous skill to have, but it doesn't mean you stop being human and having reactions to things. 'Aaaargh!' I hear myself say on numerous occasions. If I'm in adult mode, I can then choose what I do with all those feelings.

Which leads us to . . .

Be compassionate

Letting the other person be another person has additional elements to it as well. Not only do we need to learn to tolerate odd (odd to us, of course, not necessarily to them) or annoying behaviours, we also need to learn how to be more compassionate towards them as well.

Walking a mile in someone else's shoes can be fairly tough going. Trying to imagine what it must be like in someone else's head and heart can create a more compassionate view of them. You don't have to like what they do any more than you did before, but having compassion means you do understand some of the difficulty or pain they live with.

We often get so caught up in our own view of life that it's hard to see beyond the things we don't like in our families. Compassion is a good place to start.

View the world with a bit of humour

The ability to laugh at oneself and at the ridiculous things we all get up to is a quality worth hanging on to and developing. Life is serious enough as it is, and sometimes we all get just a little too solemn in our day-to-day dealings with it all. When with our families it can really seem serious and that's the time when a little humour goes a long way.

You've heard the term 'lighten up'; well, just about every one of us could afford to lighten up a lot more than we do. It's also more fun being around people who delight in what's happening around them, rather than stare grim-faced at the world.

Take responsibility for how you feel

There are common phrases that we all say at one time or another: 'He made me feel worthless'; 'She made me feel so angry'; 'They made me feel like what I had to say didn't matter.'

People's behaviour does trigger feelings in us, no question about that. But they don't *make* us feel a certain way – we *choose* how we feel. OK, OK, I can hear some of you protesting, 'Of course, people make you feel things! How can you say they don't; how can you say we choose how we feel?'

When we're little and awful things are done to us, we, of course, don't have much choice in how we feel. As we get older, however, believe it or not we can choose how we react. When we choose how we react, we choose how we feel.

If someone comes up to me and says, 'I don't like what you've done to your hair,' I can react by feeling insulted, especially if I'm already having a bad hair day. If I'm not having a bad hair day and I really like what I've done with my hair, I couldn't care less what anyone says.

I can't control what other people say or do. How I react is entirely up to me.

Apologise; admit when you are wrong

Since I was someone who was always right and hated being wrong, I had to learn how to genuinely apologise and admit my mistakes. I had spent so much time covering up or justifying what I did, that it took me a while – a long while – to realise just how powerful giving someone a heartfelt apology could be. Not only that, if I caught myself 'in the moment' as it were and held up my hand as soon as I became aware of my less than wonderful behaviour, it made a huge difference. What I discovered is that other people have an amazing capacity (as I have myself when on the receiving end of an apology) to let you off the hook.

It's when we use up a lot of energy holding on to being perfect, and therefore incapable of making mistakes, that makes other people less willing to come halfway.

What I found helpful to remember is that an apology is for the other person – it's taking care of them, not making you feel better.

Forgive

From the last chapter, of course, I have to include forgiveness. It follows on well from allowing and compassion and is an important and incredibly mature quality to develop.

Forgiving others and ourselves is indeed a way to put aside childish things and move more firmly into adulthood, no matter what your age is.

I debated whether to include patience in this list of adult behaviours. I figured if you could do a lot of the ones I have already included, by default you will have to be more patient. If you look before you leap, see other people's points of view, separate yourself from the situation, stay calm in a crisis, you will automatically be exhibiting patience. All of those things slow your response time down, or your reactive time down, and therefore, by the very nature of that, you become more thoughtful and thus more patient.

There are many more behaviours that I consider 'adult' and I'll be including them in the last two chapters. For now, however, the above list is a lot to be getting on with.

I also assume that you already do many of these behaviours. Some will feel really comfortable and you do them with ease – they are part of who you already are. If there are some on this list you haven't thought of or tried practising, now is a good time to begin.

Exercise four

Having read through the list, choose one or two new adult behaviours that you think you could start to try out on difficult family members.

Adult behaviours:

____

____

____

Who I'm going to try them out on:

____

____

____

A Heavenly Approach

When I look at the way heavenly families relate to each other one of the key things that makes a difference is that at least one or usually more family members have mature roles which can take the sting out of the other, less mature roles which other members of their family may be playing. They choose roles that help resolve problems rather than compound them.

Do you remember Anina's story from Chapter Five? That featured the sister–brother spat which resulted in Anina telling her brother to go slit his throat. I bet that you wouldn't have identified her and her family as a heavenly one. It was all pretty volatile, unkind and certainly immature. Interestingly enough, though, they are heavenly. The specific incident she describes was certainly hellish, but read on to see the heavenly outcome.

Case study: Anina's story continued

'I thought that this was completely between my brother and me. I was totally unaware the effect this was having on everyone else in the family, particularly my children. When my 14-year-old daughter came to me and said, "Mama, I can't take this any more. Stop talking to Zio Michele like that; don't say those things. Stop winding him up like you do," my other two children chipped in as well and said they felt the same way. I just hadn't seen the effect I was having. It was devastating to me to realise that something that I felt was just between

Michele and me was having such a huge impact on the family.

'My daughter also told me I had to go and apologise to Michele in front of everyone, which I did. He even said in response, "I know I get to you, but I don't know what I do."

'By her coming to me like that I saw things in a way I hadn't before. I looked at my 14-year-old daughter and realised right then she had a wisdom which I could take from her and learn.

'I know that through this something got healed between my brother and me which had festered for a long time. In the end, it didn't really matter why or where it came from; what was important is that we can be in a room together now without taking potshots at each other.'

This is what makes Anina's a heavenly family: there was a willingness to resolve a situation that could have escalated into a family feud which could have gone on and on down the generations; there was a climate created in the way the children were brought up that made it possible for them to come to Anina, knowing they would be listened to; there was a humility both in accepting fault and that everyone can learn from everyone else – it's two-way. There were open hearts.

In the next chapter will show you how to put some of these adult behaviours into practice. I'll be presenting specific hellish scenarios and a variety of options you could use to resolve them.

Health alert

I've already mentioned this in a couple of places in this chapter: adult behaviour does not mean allowing others to do you harm – emotional harm, physical harm, psychological harm. The more you practise adult behaviour, the more you will be able to separate yourself from the unhealthy aspects of your family. You will be able to see where issues could possibly be resolved.

Things to be aware of:

Be aware of when you still feel helpless and defenceless.

Be aware of areas where you still pretend.

Be aware if people in your family pretend things aren't happening when they are.

Be aware of the age you revert to when under stress.

Be aware of the reasons you took on some of your childish roles.

Be aware when you are still being childish.

Be aware of the impact your childish behaviour has on other family members.

Be aware of the wonderful childlike behaviour you are capable of.

Things you could try:

Try practising a different aspect of adult behaviour every week.

Try being more childlike.

8

How to Stop the Runaway Train

Choo, Choo, Choo

We've all been there – once we're drawn into the family dynamic there's no stopping it. Or it *feels* as though there's no stopping it. We come together to celebrate a niece's wedding or Gran's retirement party and, before we know it, all those old patterns are in full swing and there we are, playing it all out again. Like a runaway train, we're swept along on familiar tracks, little side-spurs taking us to out-of-the-way stops that no one even remembers any more.

Not only that, our thoughts can be like a runaway train as well, where we seem to have utterly no control over the speed of the hamster wheel which is going absolutely nowhere: round and round those thoughts go in an endless loop.

These thoughts take many forms. Certainly there's wishful thinking and/or dread of the next get-together. There's also replaying past ones and reliving the worst, most excruciating moments. Over and over and over again. Including replaying any arguments or unpleasant conversations that happened. Including replaying things that never got said.

The Phantom Dialogues. These are the conversations that you make up and never have. You make up what you're going to say, then you make up what the other person is going to say, then you make up your response and make up the response to the response and so on. This is part of that heroic stuff, when you finally say everything you've always wanted to.

You never have the conversations for all the reasons I wrote about earlier, but that doesn't stop you replaying these Phantom Dialogues, embellishing them, becoming even more heroic and brave, rescuing the family from itself.

A great number of your hamster-wheel thoughts are also taken up with fears of what might happen if you did do something out of the norm; if you did have the heroic outburst or even if you calmly said to family members just what was what.

Case study: Li's story continued

'I realise that I was creating a great deal of stress not just when I visited my parents, but all the time. I was frightened to tell my parents how unhappy I was they weren't proud of me when that was what I wanted more than anything. My biggest fear was that I'd finally hear what they really thought of me. Even though I'd assumed they were disappointed, I didn't think I could bear to hear it said.

'My husband finally did snap, but not in the way I had been anxious he would. He told me I had to speak to them or he would stop going with me to Sunday meals. I was surprised that the idea of going alone frightened me more than speaking to them, so I gathered my courage around me and, the very next Sunday, took them aside to tell them some of my thoughts.

'I explained to them how much their respect meant to me and that I was sad they weren't proud of me and the life I had chosen. Ma scolded me for thinking such a thing. In Chinese, of course, she told me off for being an ungrateful daughter for not realising how very satisfied she and my father were of everything I did. She even said they were a bit intimidated by all my achievements.

> 'That is just like my mother – putting me in the wrong for thinking they weren't proud, but I felt so much better afterwards because I realised that though they may have been disappointed I didn't study traditional Chinese medicine, it didn't mean they didn't respect the choices I had made.'

Big fears

Like Li, we all have fears about what might happen if we did something out of the ordinary; tried talking to someone differently, broke the rules or stepped out of our expected roles into new ones.

In no particular order of importance here are the main fears I've heard from people over the years:

Big fear number one: They'll stop loving me.

Big fear number two: They'll stop doing things for me.

Big fear number three: They'll stop respecting me.

Big fear number four: I'll trigger some cataclysmic rupture in the family.

Big fear number five: I'll be ostracised; they'll stop talking to me; they'll throw me out of the family.

Big fear number six: I'll make it worse than it already is.

Big fear number seven: I might hear things I don't want to hear.

Big fear number eight: I might say something I'll regret.

Big fear number nine: They won't forgive me.

Big fear number ten: They'll think I'm selfish.

Those are just a few; there are countless fears we all have about the breakdown of our familial relationships. Fears are another thing that throw us right back into our most vulnerable child self.

All these big fears are valid. They might happen. Every single one of them has happened in many families many times. You simply don't know and, in the not knowing, you get to stay stuck. Fears are one of the ways we keep ourselves immature: we make up these awful things that might happen and then we feed the fears. We feed them with proof we've collected, we feed them with unsubstantiated fantasies, we feed them with other people's gossip. Like those deposits in the memory bank that get bloated with 'interest', our fears get bloated as well.

Most of our fears came when we were little. Along with all the other stuff we're carrying from those early years, we've got fears to add to the pile as well. When we were very young, the fears had more validity: often children are threatened with the loss of love ('If you don't brush your teeth right now, I won't come and tuck you in'). Parents at the end of their tethers often use threats to get their kids to do what they want. Sometimes the threats have no real force behind them; they're said automatically, without thought. To a vulnerable child, however, the risk of loss of love or care is huge. Sometimes the threats do have more force behind them. There are some parents who are not only at the end of their tethers with their children's impossible behaviour, but, more importantly and tragically, they are at a loss in their own lives and so take out their bewilderment, fear and anger on the easiest target available. In both situations, the threat can feel real, and fear implanted in that way is damn hard to budge as the child gets older.

We're frightened that our parents will think of less of us; the esteem in which they hold us will be cut down to size.

Along with the love of our families, we need their esteem as well. We want them to be proud of what we do and who we are. Losing this is a daunting thought and, in many instances, stops people from truly being themselves or striking out on a path not acceptable to their parents. That was one of the torments Li experienced when she decided to train as a Western doctor instead of a traditional Chinese one. As we've seen from her case study, though, that fear was unfounded. Her parents were indeed disappointed, but once she was able to talk with them 'heart-to-heart' they told her just how proud they were of everything she had done and her successes. On the other hand, in Nisar's case the fear that he would be ostracised by his family could very well be true. His fear has a very real foundation.

If you ask most people what they want for their children, even if they are on the brink of serious 'dysfunction', they will say they want their children to be happy. Now their version of happiness might be polar opposite to what you want for your own happiness, but the point is that parents do want to see their children doing well and having good lives.

In most families you'd have to do something fairly extreme and utterly unforgivable for people to abandon their love for you. It may happen, but most of us don't turn our love on and off like a tap when it comes to family. If they genuinely love you, then it's unlikely they'll stop loving you if what you are attempting to do is create a stronger communication connection. They may be frightened themselves or anxious about any boat rocking you may start, but stop loving you . . . that's quite a leap.

Many of my fears came because there was a lot of yelling and screaming and threats when I was growing up, so I have a 'They'll be very, very angry with me' fear and it certainly seemed real to me. As did the 'I'll make it worse than it already is' one. I know exactly where that one came from to the smallest detail and I was only three. I said something to my father about my mother and all hell broke loose. I sure learnt my lesson there. Keep quiet and stay out of the line of fire.

The power of grown-up behaviour can feel like a runaway train – out of control. In some cases, it can feel as though we've been hit by the runaway train and kapow! we learn to fear.

The adult you has to take a realistic look at each situation to determine whether any of your fears are grounded or whether you are using them as an excuse not to do anything. However, so many of the fears that stop us behaving differently or trying to change the family dynamic have as much basis in truth as our wishful thinking. We let our fears run things the same way our knee-jerk reactions run things.

Exercise one

Either using the Big Fear list I've compiled, or add any of your own, identify your own biggest fears regarding your family:

My biggest fears are:

____

____

____

____

____

____

The root of these fears are:

____

____

____

____

____

____

These fears stop me saying/doing:

____

____

____

____

____

____

Putting the brakes on

For the rest of this chapter I'll be making a range of suggestions for dealing with some of the bigger issues around family events and looking at a variety of scenarios and situations from family get-togethers I've heard of over the years, or from the case studies already presented in this book. I'll show you different options that might resolve it; the operative word here being 'might'. We never know what new behaviour will create.

Each option is designed to shift the status quo. In shifting the status quo, something else might shift as well. Will they heal all rifts? Unlikely. Will they be right for everyone? Certainly not. They are designed to show you there are always different ways to handle just about every situation; whether you are able to try them out is your judgement call. My encouragement to you is to identify the ones you think suit you and give them a go.

The one option I have not included, but always remains open, is that you maintain the status quo. I hope that having got this far in the book you won't want to, but sometimes it can feel as though that's the only option you've got. What I recommend in that case is to keep on noticing: you may choose to do nothing, but that doesn't mean you have to stay unconscious. I suspect that in time the more you pay attention and notice, the more likely you will be to spot an opportunity to do something different.

We'll start with the hard stuff – those big family gatherings that seem to auger disaster.

Big events, big feelings part II

Remember way back in Chapter One I talked about how major holidays seemed to be a trigger for major family traumas and disasters? It does seem as though the conjunction of these big universal, national, religious or secular events with the coming together of family members sparks off deep emotional crises in some people. It's as though they store up their dramas till they have a familiar audience and then they seem to let rip. Quite simply, many people feel more vulnerable when the family get-together has the additional burden of even higher expectations than usual. It may be bad enough knowing your next family gathering is going to be fraught with difficulty just because they normally are, but if it's one of the big ones (New Year's or Eid al-Fitr or Thanksgiving or Christmas), it seems those difficulties are magnified by even higher expectations than normal: the pressure to be more loving, more grateful, more dutiful, more celebratory, more devout is enormous.

Naturally, occasional crises do occur by chance on big holidays. My own grandmother died on Christmas Eve one year, not a problem because we're Jewish, you might think. But since those of us who were married were married primarily to non-Jews, everyone had to leave behind their Christmas plans to attend her funeral. My grandmother was wont to make dramatic gestures, but I don't think that was her intention in dying when she did.

The pressure I'm talking about is more like one family I know who, for as long as I've known them, have one major blowout a year during Christmas, as regular as clockwork, which takes four to six months to heal before everyone is talking to each other again and stops being mad. I'm talking about another family of a former client whose members inevitably announced some dreadful news just before everyone was getting ready for evening prayers at the mosque on the major holy days. Of course, there wasn't time to do anything about it right then and there and, whatever the big news was, it would be on people's minds during prayer whether they liked it or not.

I'm talking about one family I've not met but about whom I have heard quite a bit through a mutual friend, some of whose members now take bets before a family wedding or birthday party or anniversary on who's going to proclaim what. Is sister Petra going to declare that she's getting divorced? Is cousin Eddie going to reveal he's gay after all? Is Dad going to say he has eight months to live? They apparently make a joke of it but, from what I've been told, some catastrophe unfolds right smack in the middle of the big celebrations or sadder times on a regular basis.

The big dramas seem to be the pressure valve some people need to create, but it's tough if you're on the receiving end more than if you are the one doing the 'creating'. If you are the one doing the creating, you do have to ask yourself what happens to you? If it happens more than once, it simply isn't coincidence, no matter how much you'd like to justify it as such.

If this is something that regularly happens in your family here are some suggestions. They could work equally well for the smaller get-together, but it's the big ones that for some people seem to be the worst.

Options

1. Don't go. Make an alternative plan. 'I couldn't possibly do that!' This is a cry I've heard many times when I've made the suggestion. It's what so many of you would like to do and yet you feel obligated to spend Passover or Thanksgiving or Diwali or Christmas with the very people who set your teeth on edge and after which you say 'Never again' again.

   The thing about alternative plans is to make them way ahead of time – months ahead. This way you have a goodly stretch to prepare people for your absence. It will also give you time to manage the guilt others may try to lay at your feet. There is no question that if you're someone who always shows up for everything and you decide to not turn up because you've planned something else, your actions will certainly cause a stir.

The trick is not to justify your plans, to be kind and understanding:

'I can hear how upset you are.'

'It sounds as though you're really going to miss us.'

'We're not coming this time, so we'll give you a ring during the day.'

'My brother may not like it and I can understand that; we've always been with you together.'

Notice no 'buts' in these statements. They're neutral, empathetic; there are no excuses, no rationalisations. The focus is on taking care of the other family members without giving in or defending yourself.

2. If making an alternative plan is a bridge too far, then set a time limit for your visit. Even if you've had to travel 150 miles, or even a lot more, to get there, if you let everyone know you'll only be able to stay two/three/whatever number of hours, no matter how disappointed your family members might be and how much guilt they ladle over you, you'll have 'done your duty', made your appearance and then you can make your goodbyes and your getaway.

3. See if you can avoid getting drawn into the drama, and even better if you can convince other family members not to get drawn in as well. A lot of more modern child-rearing books talk about not rewarding bad behaviour by giving children too much attention when they're being naughty and I believe the same holds true for adults. If everyone is used to crisis management

during family get-togethers then a pattern has been created that compensates the crisis-creator with loads of attention and sympathy or exasperation and frustration. Whichever emotions are being doled out, the person is still being rewarded for creating the crisis in the first place; they know that they will have their big moment in the spotlight.

What would happen if that person had no audience? What would happen if instead of feeding the problem by offering a shoulder to cry on or lots of solutions or numerous 'Oh, he didn't!', 'How terrible,' 'Poor you,' the person heard the sounds of silence? It may give you the time you need to regroup and gain more inner strength to resist the pull of the drama.

It may not.

All families 'collude' (either knowingly or unknowingly) in maintaining the status quo. If the status quo is healthy, all well and good – the collusion isn't making things worse or perpetuating hellish behaviour. If the status quo is unhealthy, then reacting to or even creating predictable dramas keeps the family dynamics in one of those endless loops. If you can steel yourself to not react as you always do to others' performances, the status quo may shift, even infinitesimally. If you and others continue to withhold your 'rewards' it may shift even more.

4. Change the venue. This is an interesting one to think about. Sometimes the same old familiar surroundings make it easier for people to act out their usual patterns of behaviour. Everyone knows their parts, they'll sit in the same chairs, hang out in the same way they always do, seek out the same 'camps' and so on.

I remember quite a few years ago a work colleague, Bev, telling me about the birthday parties that would inevitably get ruined by either her or one of her two sisters. It seemed that as soon as they got together to celebrate, one of them would announce some disaster or other: being fired, finding out a boyfriend was having an affair, the sale of a flat falling through or the third car accident that year. Bev was just as guilty of this as her sisters and they seemed to take it in turns to be in some kind of trouble. No one seemed immune to calamity.

She noticed that the birthday parties would always start out all right, with their friends and family all seemingly having a good time, but as the evenings would wear on, the parents and siblings would gravitate to the kitchen and sure enough, as other people were all chatting and eating and drinking, the bombshell would be dropped. Then the usual kerfuffle would ensue and everyone would get drawn in, once more, to whatever misfortune had befallen one of the girls, and the party atmosphere would be in shambles.

Bev decided to try something different and, at the planning stages of one of her sister's birthdays, she suggested to her mother that instead of hosting the party at home, they book a restaurant, a village hall or a church hall, as long as it was someplace different.

Amazingly, it worked. Bev said she was aware that because the immediate family couldn't do their usual congregating in the kitchen and ignoring their guests, the usual crisis announcement couldn't be made in the same way. Of course, one of them had indeed just broken up with her latest partner, but she chose not to act out in front of everyone the way everyone was used to and, although she mentioned it, it wasn't presented in the same way.

Now, this is just one example of venue changing actually working. In Bev's case, it didn't make the family different, but in changing the geography it did change the way the family behaved.

What I like about trying a different location than the family is used to is that you don't really have to do anything overtly different. You don't have to plan way ahead; you don't have to set a time limit on how long you stay; you don't even have to avoid getting drawn into the drama. You just have to change where you sit.

5. Make a decision. As a matter of fact, make just about any decision. The problem with big events is that it's easy to get on that runaway train and hang on for dear life till it crashes or screeches to a halt or goes off the rails. It's easy to let circumstances dictate what you do instead of you dictating what you do.

   When you start making decisions, you become more in charge of what happens around you instead of letting 'it' be in control of you. You could make a decision not to attend; you could make a decision to try a different role; you could make a decision to break a rule. Decisions could also include removing yourself from any family disagreements, not taking sides, letting the chips fall where they may.

   Highly recommended would be making a decision to practise any number of adult behaviours.

Exercise two

If you are part of a family that has big crises at the big events, think about the last two or three major holidays/family get-togethers and list the dramas that unfolded (or exploded):

____

____

Given just a few of the options described above, which of them might be adapted and tried out at your next big get-together?

Typical scenarios

Here are some of the situations that are typical of the fixes people find themselves in during highly fraught family get-togethers and my suggested options for resolving them.

As with the big events just dealt with, they all would require a change of behaviour and there is no guarantee this new behaviour will work; most importantly, however, they all are about doing something new.

Scenario one: Rashi's tale

I was chatting with my friend, Rashi, who felt she could never say anything to her auntie Diti because she was always the biggest help at family events. Rashi loves to take on the organising of Diwali, everyone's birthday parties, anniversaries and so on, and Auntie Diti is always right there, lending a hand with food, decorations and getting just the right music.

'I love Auntie Diti, but I don't always like her. She's a terrible gossip and stirs up trouble between all us siblings and cousins. The atmosphere can get very tense.'

Rashi's fear was that if she said anything to her aunt about her gossiping, then she would storm out in a huff and never be around to help. Then other family members would accuse Rashi of upsetting Auntie Diti and turn against her, even though many of them had complained to her about the gossiping. Rashi also thought she (Rashi) was being selfish – as though the only reason she tolerated her aunt was so she could help out at the parties.

See reality for what it is: the first thing Rashi had to accept was that this was true, at least in part. She did appreciate the help Auntie Diti gave and it was true that if she did storm out in a huff Rashi would be left doing everything herself at family dos.

What a lot of things going on at once. First, Rashi's fears at this point were all in her head. Her fears of saying something to Auntie Diti and appearing selfish stopped her doing anything. Second, there's clearly been a pattern established that Rashi and Diti do all the work and everyone else gets to enjoy it. Third, everyone in the family is caught up in the drama, because other family members go to Rashi to complain about Auntie Diti. Everyone seems to know what's going on but no one else is doing anything to change it. Fourth, what might be going on underneath? I imagine that Auntie Diti wants to feel needed, which is why she makes sure she's Rashi's right-hand woman. Of course I can't know for sure, but the gossiping could be a way of her attaching herself to other family members – gossip is often used as 'currency' to feel connected to other people.

Options:

1. Rashi could talk to one or two other family members and see how willing they would be to lend a hand at the next couple of parties. This would provide backup in case Auntie Diti really did get so upset she'd storm off. She doesn't have to tell them why she's asking for help but she'll have covered her backside just in case.

2. She could talk to every member of her family and suggest that they all agree to stop listening to the gossip and taking sides. If Auntie Diti has no audience that might stop her incessant gossiping.

3. If Rashi does decide to say something she thinks will be unpleasant to hear, she has to let Auntie Diti know how much she appreciates what she does to make the events so successful and how much of the burden she relieves from Rashi's shoulders.

4. Rashi could tell Auntie Diti the truth: that she has something to say but that she's frightened Auntie Diti will get angry and not want to be around the family any more. She could combine this with being diplomatic.

When we work up the courage to say things it often gets blurted out a bit bluntly so we can get it over with. Rashi has to decide the effect she wants to have on Auntie Diti first. In this case she wants to make sure she doesn't feel criticised but at the same time she does want Auntie Diti to know she needs to stop gossiping.

Her fear is that she'd say something like, 'Auntie Diti, no one likes all the gossiping you do. You stir things up and create bad blood between people. No one likes it but everyone's too afraid to say anything to you. You've got to stop all your interfering.'

That could certainly hasten Rashi's worst fears to become real.

This is what I recommended she say: 'Auntie Diti, you are completely indispensable to the family and we all love you. I'd be out on a limb without your help. You know, I don't think you realise just how much we care about you. And I'm not sure we realise how much you care about us. I hope you don't feel we're all taking advantage?'

And that's it. I didn't recommend she even bring up the gossiping issue. The tactic I suggested was about Auntie Diti feeling appreciated and seeing if that made any difference at all. I didn't want Rashi to bring up anything critical because that would take the pleasure out of the praise.

I did say to Rashi to see if anything shifted at all, and if not then she could gently bring up the issue by saying something along the lines of, 'Do you know, all us young people get on most of the time, but sometimes it feels as though you tell tales about us to each other and that doesn't really help. Maybe you don't realise how unhappy it makes us to think that sometimes you do spread rumours which aren't really true.'

In the first instance, it did shift things . . . for a little while. Rashi did end up using her next choice of words (having lined up two of her cousins to help at the next party, just in case). She adapted mine to suit her own style of talking, but she did eventually say something. There were some tears and a feeble attempt to defend herself, but Auntie Diti didn't storm out. Rashi kept repeating how much she cared about her and things did improve.

Rashi's attempt to change things did remind me of something crucial though. She gave her auntie lots of praise and acknowledgement, but the bit I left off was that once is hardly likely to shift things permanently. If family dynamics are so well entrenched, because they've been going on for years, doing something just once will not make it all go away. Occasionally, it can happen, but it's back to the wishful thinking again.

OK, you stepped out of the norm, did something different and now it will all fix itself and everyone will 'get' what they need to do differently and you won't have to make yourself uncomfortable any more. It doesn't work that way. You may have to repeat new behaviour half a dozen times before anything changes, or changes permanently. With any new skill, you don't learn it in one go; you have to keep practising. With behaviour change, you're not only dealing with your behaviour, but with everyone else's as well.

Once you see that something you do has had an effect, you need to embed it so that it becomes more the norm than the old behaviour.

Scenario two: Grandma's tale

Recently, I overheard three elderly women have a complaint fest. It was hard not to eavesdrop, so I did since they were so wrapped up in exchanging their tales of woe they didn't notice me with a big ear tuned in to their conversation.

One woman, in particular, repeated her misery over and over again; every time one of the others told her story she would immediately come in with, 'Complaints? I have complaints I can tell you. "Who's going to drive Grandma home?" "Who's going to drive Grandma home?" Every time the same thing.'

This went on for some time, and I got more of a gist of what happens when she visits her daughter, son-in-law and grandsons. Here's my version of what could ensue when she's ready to go home:

'Who's going to drive Grandma home?'

Silence.

'Someone has to take Grandma home.'

'Not me, I did it last time.'

'The game's just started; I'll drive her later.'

'It's all right. I'll just take a taxi home. Does anyone have the name of a taxi firm?'

'Mother, you're not taking a taxi; one of the boys will drive you home, won't you? Don't spoil everything now.'

'Oh, Ma!'

'I don't mind taking a taxi. You know I don't like being out after dark.'

'You're not out after dark, Mum. You're here with us. Oh, forget it. I'll drive you home.'

'No, you've done enough today with all the cooking. Let one of my grandsons drive me home.'

Get the picture? This dialogue (like a bad endless vaudeville routine) could go on forever, and has surely been repeated in some form or another for just about ever. Everyone knows their lines and it plays out like a medieval tapestry full of story and symbolism.

However, any one of the players could change their lines, which would change the routine and the outcome.

On the surface, Grandma looks like the innocent victim – an aged 'pass the parcel' – but life and families are more complicated than that. Not too much innocence in this family scenario. If you were her, what could you do differently? When you're in the midst of this kind of scenario, it's hard to think of what else you could do to change the family script, so I'll give you a few ideas, all of which would change things.

Options:

1. On arrival, Grandma could announce the time she wants to be home and ensure that someone agrees then to drive her home at the appointed time.

2. She could come armed with a taxi firm number or, better yet, have already booked a taxi to pick her up at her chosen time.

3. Knowing that there's going to be the usual squabble, she could pick her moment to plonk herself down in front of the 'game', fall asleep and snore really loudly.

4. She could say, 'That's OK then, why don't I just stay the night?'

She could do just about anything to change the old routine. Sadly, I imagine that if I sat next to those elderly women again, I'd still hear the same woeful stories just as I had overheard them before.

Scenario three: Steven's story continued

Steven was certainly in a difficult position. His parents would get drunk at every family get-together and, as we have seen earlier, he and his brothers would spend a lot of time in Fantasyland, hoping that each time it wouldn't happen. His fears were so numerous he almost couldn't keep track of them: he was afraid he'd make it worse and they'd get more drunk to spite him; he was afraid he'd say something so horrible they'd never forgive him; he was afraid if he really confronted them, his only option would be to never see them again till they got sober.

There's no question that when you deal with family members who have addictions, that adds a layer of complication to the proceedings. The problem – in the tiniest nutshell possible – is that when someone has an addiction, their main relationship is with whatever it is they are addicted to and not with the people around them. This is why wishful thinking is so prevalent with families affected by addiction; they want to be more important than the addiction and they aren't. This can really throw people back into immature feelings and behaviour because it feels as though they are in a position of complete powerlessness.

Working with Steven, we looked at some tricky options for him and his brothers.

Options:

1. There is always the 'intervention' route, which requires advice and support from one of the addiction recovery organisations. Intervention tackles the problem head-on and does mean that the family has to be in agreement about this course of action and be prepared to put in time, energy, possible heartache and great courage to make it happen. Steven felt he couldn't consider this as a first option.

2. He could choose to see them only at times when he knew they'd be sober – mornings and afternoons seemed a relatively safe bet, certainly a safer bet than going out with them. This would mean no confrontation, no talking about the issues, no chance of resolution. What this would do is allow Steven to see his parents on safe ground. It also meant Steven would then have to choose not to go to the big family occasions where drink flowed freely.

3. He could go to the big, drink-flowing family events and leave as soon as he saw his parents getting drunk.

I don't want to imply that these options would be easy, but the key here is to help Steven (or you, if you are in a similar situation) to feel less helpless and less victimised by the situation.

Scenario four: Christine's story continued

Christine had to get 'back to basics'. She was so focused on what her brother-in-law Geoff did that she lost sight of what made hers a close family in the first place. She could see that the fight she had with her mother and sister at her cousin's graduation was very childish, but she still couldn't find a way out of the emotional rut they had all got into.

She herself admitted how difficult she found it to identify anything positive about Geoff – she could only see the negative side of things. Even when she grudgingly recognised some useful qualities, she needed to qualify them at the same time.

The family was squabbling amongst themselves, and family gatherings, which used to be quite pleasant, were now uneasy and dissatisfying. What also seemed clear was that everyone seemed paralysed to change anything to get the family out of the mess they found themselves in.

Time to try something different.

The first thing was that Christine had to accept that if the dynamics were going to change, someone was going to have to appoint themselves the 'dynamics adjuster' because things weren't going to change on their own. Reluctantly, she knew it had to be her.

Next, we looked at what she might be able to try to kick-start some new dynamics.

Options:

1. Although in an ideal world I'd recommend she apologise to Geoff, knowing that might be too difficult, I suggested she apologise to Lisa, for not being more welcoming.

2. She could ask Geoff's advice about something that she knows he knows a thing or two about. She was already annoyed that he seemed to be throwing his weight around and thought he'd really lord it over her if she went to him for advice, but I asked her to consider the fact that maybe he was bossy because he felt insecure around her close-knit family and this was the only way he knew to express himself. By making him feel needed, even in small ways, it might mitigate his need to bully his way in.

3. It seemed clear to me that her mother, in particular, felt caught in the middle. My next option was to make a 'pact' with her mother before the next family event that no matter what happened, the two of them would not take sides, make any snide comments or criticise Geoff in front of anyone else in the family.

4. An option that required some forethought was to anticipate what Geoff might do which would get up people's noses and to pre-empt it. For instance, Christine

> knew it rubbed everyone up the wrong way that Geoff made a big deal of paying for the first round of drinks whenever there was a family meal at a pub – her father liked to do that and felt his position had been usurped. Instead of Dad feeling hurt and everyone else resenting Geoff for taking over (as they saw it), an alternative could be to tell Geoff that Dad would get the first round, but, of course they all hoped Geoff would get the second round. What Christine wanted to do was to tell Geoff, 'Stop interfering in how things have always been done and let Dad get the drinks!' The new version would have to sound more like, 'Geoff, I hope you don't mind, but Dad's going to get the first round tonight, but we'll all hold you to the second round.'

In each of these scenarios, there are any number of options our protagonists could try. They might work, they might not. The important thing is that the options mean trying out something different from what has always been done. One thing any of these options might very well do is to make you feel better about yourself because you are trying something new and initiating changes.

To stay or not to stay

As well as the option to maintain the status quo, there is the other end of the spectrum, which is the option to walk away. As I've said, Fred and I walked away from his parents, and I know a number of people who have chosen that option as a way of protecting themselves.

This is *not* the same as not talking to someone, which is immature behaviour and, once again, perpetuates stuck relationships. Walking away is a difficult choice because you walk away from hope that it will change, that you will get on better with the trickier family members who make the get-togethers so intolerable.

The decision has to come as a last resort, after you have tried as many different ways of making it better as possible. Of course, if you are being harmed in any way, then walking away is a first resort. However, in my experience, there are many steps that can and should happen in most situations before you say, 'I can no longer be with my family.'

Walking away doesn't have to be unequivocal, it doesn't have to be forever and it doesn't have to be done in a way that creates even more drama than may already exist. There should be no ultimatums, threats or bribes ('I'll stay if . . . '). Walking away may also mean walking away from selected family members even though the result may be that you no longer attend family get-togethers. You could still have good relationships with those people you care about, instead of dumping them all because of one or two.

Now I know that can be tricky in and of itself. A friend said that when she tried to stop going to the big family gatherings, she was the one who was given an ultimatum that her immediate family expected her to be there no matter how much she disliked her uncle ('He's so slimy,' she said). It was a choice that in the end she couldn't make because she couldn't bear the thought of not having anything to do with her close family. So she continued to go to the get-togethers but tried the 'I'm only staying a couple of hours' option and her parents found that an acceptable compromise.

Having the conversations with the people who really matter is essential, so that you can articulate your feelings and your decision, and they can attempt to understand what's going on for you.

If you find that you can't cope with a face-to-face encounter, writing a letter is the next best option (please no email!), where you can take the time to get your thoughts clear.

A note about letter-writing. There is a danger that you may

want to vent all your feelings on the written page because it feels safer. Don't.

Well, let me amend that. Here's something I used to do at the suggestion of my own therapist that I have passed on to some of my clients as well. I find it works a treat. Write two letters.

One letter is everything you want to say, unedited, unbridled, let 'em rip stuff. Everything, however unkind, angry, accusing. Vent. Read it out loud. Then rip it up. That letter isn't going anywhere.

The next letter is the one you'll send, once you've had a chance to let off all that steam, articulated all those feelings. The 'real' letter should be calmer, more considerate of the recipient's feelings and kinder. A letter, where as I mentioned earlier, you can get your thoughts clear, but without the drama and finger-pointing.

I'm not a great fan of the telephone because you can't see people's faces and respond to them appropriately. So choose the 'medium' and the 'option' that might get the best results.

However, before you decide that walking away is your only option, read the next section.

Families *sans frontières*

Fred is a fiddler. No, not a violin player; he likes to fiddle with clothes. It's his real-life job, so when we're about to go out or even when we're walking in the street, he'll lean over and fiddle with the collar of my blouse, or fiddle with the way I've tied a scarf, or rolled my sleeves. Because of our closeness, without thinking or needing to ask permission, he'll enter my personal space to fiddle. In other words, he crosses my boundaries. Just as I cross his to give a kiss or a squeeze.

Most people who are close cross each other's boundaries all the time. Scooping up a small child and smooching them, walking arm in arm, giving cuddles and other ways of showing affection require us to cross another person's boundaries. This is also what happens when someone is violent and does physical harm to someone else. Physical boundaries are something everyone knows about, even if they are different in different cultures. Things such as hand-holding or other outward manifestations of affection are acceptable in some cultures and not in others, and there are hundreds of examples of how something taken for granted in one part of the world is completely unacceptable elsewhere.

Even given that, however, our personal space is ours and, in essence, we give others permission to cross our boundaries by the types of relationships we have with them. We all know what it's like ('Uncomfortable!', 'Yucky!', 'How dare they!') when someone we don't like or haven't given tacit permission to crosses our boundary and 'invades' our personal space.

It can be equally uncomfortable and yucky when someone says or does something that affects our emotions – they criticise us when we didn't ask for their opinion, or they unintentionally hurt our feelings by saying something out of line.

Here's the crux of the matter: the thing about families, both heavenly and hellish, is that boundaries can easily get blurred. When we're close to other people, it's easy to forget that what's theirs is definitely and solely theirs, not ours. Many family members kind of have this unspoken (and probably unconscious) belief that 'what's yours is mine'. In other words, they don't have any boundaries around feelings and behaviour or even people and things.

Having strong, clearly defined boundaries and setting them for other people is essential for effective communication and even better for really good relationships.

Stepping over the line

Every one of you will have dozens of examples of family members, including yourself, who have stepped over the line, trampled some boundaries and indeed acted as though 'what's yours is mine':

'Without permission, my mother rifles through my luggage whenever I come to stay, and then has the chutzpah to comment on the contents.'

'If my son doesn't like the arrangements one of us has made about an upcoming celebration, he'll change them without asking anyone how they feel about it, and then he tells us what he's done.'

'Because I have a bigger car, my sister demands that I chauffeur her and her brood whenever the family meets up.'

'We've learnt not to tell my father *anything* in confidence. Practically the second it's out of our mouths he goes and tells everyone else.'

'My niece is always telling people secrets in strict confidence, except at the end of every party or whatever, everyone's been told a different version and everyone's been sworn to secrecy. We're all just as bad because we all start telling each other the secrets she's told us in confidence.'

'We don't know how to show affection in my family, so we all kind of ridicule and make fun of each other which I guess is a way of loving.'

'My daughter embarrasses me by the way she'll coyly hit other people in the family up for a "loan" which I know (and she knows and everyone else knows) *I'll* end up paying them back.'

'My uncle wreaks havoc at family dos by giving his – usually negative – opinions about any of the major decisions one of us has made.'

One boundary crossing I've heard so many times I think it must be universal is about family mythology. You know, it's the carting out of embarrassing stories about one family member or another and repeatedly retelling these stories to all and sundry. They get embellished at each retelling and naturally any newcomer into the family has to be regaled with them over and over.

All of these are examples of boundary crossings: of deliberately or unconsciously disregarding other people's personal emotional space. This kind of disregard is so common in families that, although it can feel embarrassing, annoying, anger-inducing, it also feels terribly and depressingly normal. So normal, in fact, that it would feel incredibly awkward or even wrong to try to fortify the trampled boundaries.

Well, if you want to survive more of your family get-togethers, fortify them you must.

Good fences make good neighbours for a good reason

Fences are a clear and practical way of defining a boundary or border. That way there shouldn't be any disputes about who owns what and who's responsible for what.

Neighbours can agree to cross each other's boundaries, even do things for each other that would mean continually crossing over those borders, but all the while those fences are there, everyone knows what's what.

Not so clear with families, is it? We can't walk around with little signs saying 'This far and no farther, Aunt Betty,' 'Cross at your peril, Cousin Len' or 'Keep your distance, Mum,' no matter how much we wish we could. So this means that the boundaries have to be set by the words that come out of your mouth, despite what you might be thinking in your head.

Here's what I mean:

What you might like to say	What you might try saying
Stop doing that!	It makes me uncomfortable when you tease me like that.
Who are you to tell me what to do?	I know you're trying to be helpful, but I'd prefer to make the decision on my own.
Why don't you mind your own business?	I seriously would prefer not to talk about this right now, and I'd really like you to respect that.
Just leave me alone!	I'm feeling a bit sensitive right now, so I think it would help if you left me alone for a bit.
Are you out of your mind!	I'm concerned about what you're thinking of doing. I'm wondering if it would be helpful to talk it through a little more before you make a final decision.
Just keep out of this, will you!	I think this is between me and my brother, and is probably best sorted out between the two of us.

If you notice, column one is full of popcorn statements which also make the other person wrong, for whatever it is they're doing. In the second column the statements are much softer, less confrontational and the speaker isn't accusing anyone of anything. Indeed, the speaker is taking responsibility for how they feel and what they'd like to happen. The second column is gentler, kinder and more willing to allow the other person some dignity.

It might seem stilted at first to use such proscribed language, but let me tell you, the popcorn statements are even more proscribed and don't get anyone anywhere. They make things worse and perpetuate more of those endless communication loops.

Here's another really good example from a couple I worked with many years ago, Omar and Agnes. With minimal input from me they came up with their own boundary-setting solution about family get-together nightmares they experienced many times.

Omar and Agnes had a large house so were often 'elected' to host family gatherings such as parties, picnics, Sunday lunches and other larger holiday celebrations. They quite enjoyed it, up to a point. What they didn't like and didn't seem able to stop was the fact that many family members would come . . . and stay. They saw the extra bedrooms and would descend on Omar and Agnes with the assumption they would be welcome, which they usually were. Except that when they stayed, they kind of just 'hung out', expecting to be taken care of. They didn't help with the cooking or cleaning or other chores that help keep a large house humming.

At first, Omar and Agnes felt guilty that they resented their nearest and dearest so much; then they finally got so fed up with these invasions that they began declining being hosts to family events. Then they felt as though they were missing out because they really did love having their family all around them. They couldn't see a way out – it seemed to them they either had to put up with their family taking advantage of their hospitality or not see them at all.

As I say, just through talking it over, they came up with one of the best boundary-setting answers to this perennial problem that I highly recommend to anyone in a similar dilemma. The very next time they were nominated as hosts they said how delighted they were and first they asked each of the worst 'culprits' whether they were planning to stay over (they had never done this in the past, so they never knew exactly how many would be overnight guests). Then they assigned each guest a task: two would be in charge of organising the washing-up; two would be in charge of making sure the main living areas were neat and tidy; three or four would be in charge of organising the main meals; others were told about looking after the little ones; and a couple were even on laundry detail.

The transformation only took two or three family get-togethers for it to work quite smoothly. Omar and Agnes certainly stopped resenting all the family that came to dinner and stayed, and they stopped feeling guilty about assigning tasks. Everyone shared in making the family get-togethers fun and fair.

Boundary setting, as with so much in this book, takes doing over and over again. Eventually, you will find that your mouth will begin to feel more comfortable finding your own way of saying what needs to be said, while taking care of both yourself and the other family members.

A family get-together doesn't have to feel like a runaway train; if there are great dramas, they don't have to be indulged in or allowed to get even more dramatic. If boundaries get crossed, you can establish a border guard to create some space where real dialogue might be possible.

Things to be aware of:

Be aware of what the runaway train looks and feels like at some of your hellish get-togethers.

Be aware of the fears that stop you behaving differently with your family.

Be aware of the dramas you or other members of your family create at the big (or even small) events.

Be aware of any boundaries that get crossed at your family get-togethers, including any you might step over.

Things you can try:

Identify your fears and see if you can do a 'reality check' on how valid they still are.

Try any one of the many options I suggested to calm the drama and take the force out of the crises that explode at your family gatherings.

Equally, try any of the options I suggest to mitigate the difficulties at your most difficult and trying family events.

Practise setting clear boundaries for members of your family.

Practise more adult behaviours.

9

Heaven Is As Good As It Gets: A Happier Family . . . Maybe

Are we there yet?

If you have a history of unhappy, even dreadful, family get-togethers, you need a strategy to cope better. By now, I hope you will have uncovered, dissected, picked apart and investigated quite a bit of the dynamics that happen at your family get-togethers. You will probably have identified the roles you and others play in keeping these dynamics stuck, and the rules and patterns that can make communication difficult. You'll have examined where you and others play out childish behaviour at your family events and how you and others can get 'got' by the same old 'performances' and thoughtless talk. You may have been able to identify how some of these behaviours have been embedded in your family for generations and without doubt you will have understood the degree of wishful thinking and expectations you have around your family.

Part of this process will have been to see where you aren't authentic, where you pretend and where you perhaps hold on to ancient grudges and hurtful memories. In turn, I hope that you will have seen where your family dynamics are healthy and flourishing; where you and others do act like adults and where you are able to be your authentic self. By now, you should have a pretty good idea that there are options available to you and that you can redraw what your family 'territory' looks and feels like.

In this final chapter, I will show you how to put it all together: how to gather together all the insights, techniques and new behaviours suggested in previous chapters into an actual plan. By now, you will have certainly realised just how unconscious some of your (and other family members') behaviour has been. By getting conscious, knowing there are always options, you can create your own survival strategy.

Before we settle down to strategise, there's one more bit of consciousness raising I want to include here, and that's to do with the way many families argue, or rather what it is that many families – perhaps even yours – argue about.

Big stuff, little stuff

Many families, including my own, and probably yours, are guilty (if that's the right word) of arguing about the unimportant, or less important, because we can't – or don't know how to – talk about what really might be going on. Most of us don't talk about the big stuff; we skirt around the edges in the hopes that other people will figure out what's going on and do something about it. We want people to read our minds so we don't have to say how we really feel and become vulnerable and expose ourselves to one of our big fears.

Often, it's because we, and our families, don't really know what the big stuff is and so the little, petty stuff seems real and we can let rip about who was supposed to bring the extra cutlery and didn't; or who didn't get invited to whose wedding; or 'For Pete's sake, why do you always drum your fingers on the table like that when you know I don't like it?' Startling, in a way, how we'll generally go for the little stuff and argue till the cows come home rather than face the big stuff where we might have to really get at the heart of our distress.

Years ago, I was working with a psychotherapy client who had a disastrous history of family get-togethers, especially in the relationship she had with her mother: every single time they got together, at whatever happy or sad occasion, her mother would criticise her about what she hadn't done or wasn't doing better. My client would end up defending herself, yelling at her mother and retreating to her old bedroom to cry. Her sisters would take sides, her father would hide in the shed and she'd usually end up leaving without saying goodbye, driving off in a huff. The focus was so much on the little stuff that my client and her family couldn't seem to get at the heart of what was really going on, which was more about acceptance and need than about all the stuff that was getting criticised.

When we opened this particular can of worms, we did spend some time rooting through the past to put things in context, but I was far more interested in what she could do in the present to change things. She genuinely didn't think she could confront her mother and other family members about the big issues, but we created a strategy which she felt she could try. Before her mother could open her mouth, my client would pre-empt her: 'Before you say anything, Mum, I should let you know that I haven't lost any weight, I'm still with the same boyfriend, I didn't get the promotion yet and I'm keeping my hair colour.' Her mother was so taken aback that she began to justify and defend herself and my client ended up taking the initiative, making it all right for her mother and, for once, not winding up sobbing. After she had done this a couple of times, she did feel able to introduce some of her own deeper feelings about feeling overly criticised and not accepted; from there things slowly improved and others in the family, too, weren't so afraid to bring more sensitive issues into the open.

That was certainly one technique which helped open things up so that the big stuff wasn't constantly overshadowed by the little stuff.

Next, I have a couple of conversations that also illustrate other ways to stop the runaway train and get the family talking about the important and vital issues rather than edging away from them. First, I give versions where it's all about the little stuff, then I follow each one with healthier and more adult versions.

Version one:

Family member 1: 'Why did you slam the door like that?'

You: 'I didn't slam the door.'

Family member 1: 'Yes, you did. You did it deliberately because you know I have a headache.'

You: 'Oh, come on. I didn't know your headache was that bad, and I didn't slam the door.'

Family member 1: 'Yes, you did. You always do things like that to annoy me.'

Family member 2: 'Listen, you two, would you just stop this right now. I've had about enough.'

Family member 1: 'Oh, another country heard from. Who asked you to butt in?'

Family member 2: 'This is getting ridiculous. Would everyone just calm down?'

Family member 1 and you: 'We are calm.'

Popcorn statements strewn all over the place; arguing about nothing, other people getting drawn in. What might be going on here? With all the back and forth, the big stuff could be anything. Clearly, it's easier to squabble about something as inconsequential as a door slam and turn it into something huge.

I have seen it, I have experienced it, I have even been a perpetrator. Latch on to something and hang on because it feels real. The effort to stop and really see what's going on is a skill that very few of us learn when we're young, particularly if the behaviour we've seen 'modelled' isn't very mature either. First, there's the skill of getting some emotional distance from the small stuff which triggered the big reaction in the first place; enough distance to see that you have reacted without thought. Second is the skill – even harder – to figure out what might lie beneath the reaction. The next skill is to slow the conversation down long enough to be able to introduce your insight and make it accessible to whoever you're having the argument with.

The final skill is to see if between you and the other person (or people) you can all arrive at a resolution.

Let's give it a go:

Version two:

Family member 1: 'Why did you slam the door like that?'

You: 'I didn't slam the door.'

Family member 1: 'Yes, you did. You did it deliberately because you know I have a headache.'

You: 'Oh, come on. I didn't know your headache was that bad, and I didn't slam the door.'

Family member 1: 'Yes, you did. You always do things like that to annoy me.'

Family member 2: 'Listen, you two, would you just stop this right now? I've had about enough.'

You: 'OK, OK, let's hold on a minute, everyone, before this all gets out of hand. Maybe I did slam the door without thinking, and I'm sorry.'

Family member 1: 'You do it all the time.'

You: 'I'm going to be honest, I truly hadn't realised I did it so much; I really will be more careful in the future. And I can see where hearing the two of us bicker could be incredibly annoying.'

Family member 2: 'Well, it's not so bad.'

Family member 1: 'We weren't bickering.'

You: 'Actually, I think we bicker a lot. Neither of us likes it much, yet we seem to keep doing it.'

Family member 1: 'Are you saying it's my fault?'

You: 'It's nobody's fault. Listen, I think we've got into a habit of annoying each other, when probably what's going on is that we just wish we were more considerate to each other. I know, when we all get together, I sometimes feel so stressed I probably don't notice whether you or anyone else has a headache.'

Family member 1: 'Possibly. It isn't always easy when there are so many of us together.'

Family member 2: 'You can say that again! I just want everything to go smoothly and I hate it when people quarrel. I want to hide till it's all over.'

Family member 1: 'Me too, which is probably why I've got a headache.'

Exercise one

What could you say now to wrap it up and resolve the squabble?

You:

____

____

____

____

____

Another one? Let's up the stakes, shall we?

Version one:

Family member 1: 'Isn't it lovely having everyone together? It's been far too long. Why don't we do this more often?'

Family member 2: 'We're doing it now. Why can't that be good enough for you?'

Family member 1: 'I'm not complaining. I'm just saying it's nice when we all get together.'

You: 'We all live so far away; it isn't always easy to manage it.'

Family member 1: 'Why are you all ganging up on me? I'm happy to see all of you.'

Family member 3: 'Yes, why are you making such a big deal? It's not a big deal. We're all here, so let's enjoy each other's company.'

You: 'We're not making a big deal, I just don't like to feel criticised for not getting together more often.'

Family member 1: 'Oh, for Christ's sake, I'm not criticising anyone. Can't we all just settle down, get the food on the table and eat dinner?'

Family member 2: 'I'm not hungry.'

Family member 3: 'This is silly. Come on, everyone, stop acting so childish and let's have a drink.'

Family member 4: 'That's your solution for everything.'

Family member 3: 'I'm sorry, what are you trying to say?'

Family member 4: 'I'm not *saying* anything, but alcohol doesn't solve anything.'

Family member 3: 'Are you saying I'm an alcoholic?'

You shake your head, sighing but staying silent.

Family member 2: 'What's *your* problem?'

Family member 5, who's just walked in: 'What's going on here? You could cut the air with a knife.'

Family member 1: 'All I said was how nice it was to have everyone together and now everyone's spoilt it all.'

This 'conversation' has happened before, in some guise or another, and everyone knows their parts well. There are so many subtexts, hidden agendas, guilts and expectations that it takes literally no time before the script is being played out and the players are fulfilling their roles to perfection.

Let's see what 'You' could do to change the family dynamics.

Version two:

Family member 1: 'Isn't it lovely having everyone together. It's been far too long. Why don't we do this more often?'

Family member 2: 'We're doing it now. Why can't that be good enough for you?'

Family member 1: 'I'm not complaining. I'm just saying it's nice when we all get together.'

You: 'We all live so far away; it isn't always easy to manage it.'

Family member 1: 'Why are you all ganging up on me? I'm happy to see all of you.'

Family member 3: 'Yes, why are you making such a big deal? It's not a big deal. We're all here, so let's enjoy each other's company.'

You: 'We're not making a big deal, I just don't like to feel criticised for not getting together more often.'

Family member 1: 'Oh, for Christ's sake, I'm not criticising anyone. Can't we all just settle down, get the food on the table and eat dinner?'

Family member 2: 'I'm not hungry.'

Family member 3: 'This is silly. Come on, everyone, stop acting so childish and let's have a drink.'

Family member 4: 'That's your solution for everything.'

Family member 3: 'I'm sorry, what are you trying to say?'

Family member 4: 'I'm not *saying* anything, but alcohol doesn't solve anything.'

Family member 3: 'Are you saying I'm an alcoholic?'

You (hint, hint, time to intervene): 'I think we've all got off to a rather bad start here, and I for one didn't help. The fact is I do feel guilty for not making more of an effort and I know I'm sensitive about it.'

Family member 1: 'I really wasn't criticising you.'

You: 'I realise that now. I know you're just happy we're all here. I think we all got a little carried away.'

Family member 3: 'Well, I don't like being accused of being an alcoholic.'

Family member 4: 'I didn't say you were an alcoholic, I just think —'

You, interrupting: 'Perhaps it sounded that way, or perhaps we're all feeling a bit sensitive and guilty that this is the first time we've been together for at least six months. Why don't I start the apologies, because I probably overreacted?'

Family member 2: 'Me, too. And I really am hungry.'

Family member 5, entering: 'Have I interrupted something?'

Exercise two

Round it off.

You:

____
____
____
____
____

The 'You' character in each of these conversations was the one who had to take the initiative in order to create a different dynamic between the other 'players'. 'You' had to change the script in order to change the outcome.

The trick with the big stuff is that you don't have to do major archaeology here. You don't have to figure out the depths of people's feelings or motivations. As a matter of fact, I'd advise against it. You don't have to, at this juncture, get into the really deep stuff at all. If you handle one get-together more effectively, then at the next one (perhaps even having a few 'adult' conversations with individuals before the next event), you will be able to introduce some of the more complex and 'heavier' issues. If we use the above example, the next layer down could be about alcohol or how some family members feel as though they aren't appreciated for the efforts they do make.

The skill, as you will know by now, is to avoid making others wrong, apologise if appropriate, see the situation from many points of view and allow other people their own feelings without (too much) judgement. You should avoid the pitfalls of the old family patterns by recognising the little stuff for what it is: a very effective if ineffectual way of keeping yours and other people's true feelings at bay.

Exercise three

Take a family get-together where you know that the focus was on the little stuff so the big stuff could stay hidden, unspoken and, therefore, not dealt with.

Family get-together little stuff:

____

____

____

____

____

Now identify the big stuff it was covering up.

Family get-together big stuff:

____

____

____

____

____

Finally, is there anything you could have done or said to get your family off the little stuff and at least beginning to acknowledge some of the bigger issues?

What I might have been able to say:

____

____

____

____

____

This process is one that would be well worth doing after your next few family get-togethers. Even if you feel you're not up to trying to stop the runaway train, there is no reason why you can't examine it retrospectively to see (having got some physical distance from it) if there was anything you could have done that might have slowed it down, if not outright stopped it.

The heavenly family quiz

As I have said a number of times throughout this book, heavenly families are no different from hellish ones in that they still have all the same issues, have all the same jealousies and resentments, have roles and rules and patterns and immature behaviours. However, they do have a whole lot of other qualities as well that create healthier, more enjoyable family get-togethers.

The following quiz lists the prime virtues of heavenly families. Tick the boxes and score two points for every quality you know the *majority* of your family possesses. If you believe your family is on the 'road' to acquiring a particular virtue, score one point.

What, if any of this, happens at your family get-togethers?

	2 points	1 point
Individuals with significant influence within the family practise adult behaviour more often than not.	☐	☐
Family members have a desire to understand the big stuff and don't get diverted by the small stuff, except occasionally, because they're only human after all.	☐	☐
People have a respect and regard for the individual members of the family for who they are.	☐	☐
The above means that they have an aptitude for letting other people be who they are without trying to control them.	☐	☐

	2 points	1 point
A majority of family members share a sense of humour and an ability to laugh at the absurdities they and others in the family do.	☐	☐
People don't turn a crisis into a drama.	☐	☐
Family members listen to each other; really listen and hear what each other is saying, even if it makes them uncomfortable.	☐	☐
Relatives have time for each other.	☐	☐
The family community show their authentic selves more than they hide them.	☐	☐
People know they can't resurrect and reconstruct the past.	☐	☐
Individuals make decisions that benefit the whole.	☐	☐
Family members know how to ask for support from each other (and from outside the family as well) and are not too afraid to show their vulnerability.	☐	☐
Staying stuck feels more uncomfortable than dealing with the difficult issues.	☐	☐
People know when to quit.	☐	☐
Family members forgive and move on.	☐	☐

	2 points	1 point
Family members live in home, not alien, territory most of the time.	☐	☐
People don't overindulge in harmful gossip or spread wounding rumours about each other.	☐	☐
People 'own up' when something is their fault and are able to apologise with ease.	☐	☐

Total points: ___________

You may want to break your family into small chunks and have the quiz relate to the various chunks. It may be that in one chunk, your family scores quite high, whereas in another, it may score low. You may find that certain get-togethers score higher because the family dynamics aren't so stuck.

The idea is to give you a tool to 'measure' how well you and your family relate during your family get-togethers. The important thing at this point is get a feel for where the gaps are.

Here's an analysis of the scores:

26 – 36 points

Family heaven, without a doubt. With a score this high, your family communicates well and the dynamics within the family are vibrant and always developing. People have a high level of awareness of themselves and each other and most family difficulties will invariably be resolved. Family members care for and respect each other.

I'm betting your family get-togethers are usually loads of fun and that most of you are adept at supporting and encouraging each other. You enjoy each other's unique personalities and are proud to be part of your family.

Carry on doing whatever it is you're doing because you've probably got the right balance to keep growing as a healthy family.

16 – 25 points

You're right in the middle, where I suspect most families lie. Not heavenly but not totally hellish. There is enough awareness to know that there are areas in your family relationships that 'work' well and areas that are stuck and where you and a number of your family members need to practise new behaviours in order to shift the unhelpful status quo during family get-togethers. This will require a commitment to try new ways of communicating with each other and a determination to practise a lot more adult behaviour to break the patterns which are familiar to most of you.

At this point, I hope and trust you will have identified some of the simpler things you could do to start nudging the family away from its unsupportive and difficult behaviour towards a healthier way of being.

5 – 15 points

It's probably not too much fun at your family get-togethers. I imagine that many of the roles and rules most of you follow are somewhat calcified and probably feel immovable. The communication between family members is most likely poor and relationships are also probably divisive and volatile. You and others may keep your heads below the parapet (anything for a peaceful life), but this also means you cannot be your authentic self and must therefore spend considerable time pretending and/or stuck in wishful thinking.

It's time for a radical rethink, as they say in the business world. If you are a lone voice, you will have to accept and commit to being responsible for initiating your own shifts in behaviour and help others to make changes as well. If you know there are people in the family who share your outlook, you will need to enlist them in your new 'scheme', which would make success that much more likely.

You may decide that the effort is too great and chances of success too remote; therefore, another option is to walk away from your family get-togethers, if not your family in total.

Below 5 points

Get out now. I'm serious. If your family get-togethers have almost no redeeming features, this is doing your emotional, psychological and physical health no good at all; you are being harmed by being in such a damaging and unwholesome environment.

You have to ask yourself why you believe you need to stay in such a risky atmosphere and what fantasies you are hanging on to that will never, ever come true.

You do not have to completely walk away from every family member, but you need to stay clear of family gatherings because unless a miracle happens (see 'Culture change' below), then you are keeping your own self stuck and endangering your own well-being.

When I was putting together the quiz Fred said, 'This is going to make a lot of people depressed, isn't it?' Perhaps, but my feeling is that, even before reading this book, you already knew how bearable or unbearable your family get-togethers tend to be and if they are more on the unbearable end of the spectrum, then being depressed about your family is nothing new.

Reading this book, however, will most likely have put your family dynamics in sharper relief and given you not too many places to hide or carry on pretending. You will know that wishful thinking isn't going to change anything, nor is simply making 'them' wrong and you right, going to shift anything either.

I hope the opposite to depressed has happened by now – that you can see that there are some simple tools and techniques you could start practising to make your family get-togethers better.

Culture change

This is a very popular phrase that's used in business when the top bananas see that profits are down or morale is low or economic imperatives are putting pressure on the company to make significant changes. Then they sit round a table and decide that their company needs a big 'culture change' to get it all working again. It's a lot more complex than that, but the idea, of course, is that if things aren't going so well, then major change has to take place.

The only problem is that people find it incredibly difficult to accept and integrate major changes all in one gulp, which is how many organisations function: create a whole new way of operating, tell the employees about it (how wonderful it's all going to be in this glowing new future) and expect them all to fall in line. Therein lies disaster because these one-gulp operations can't and don't work because people – except in very rare occasions – don't respond to major changes they themselves haven't initiated. People don't like imposed change and they will resist it like mad.

It is the same with families. If you have particularly difficult family members, they aren't going to jump up and down with glee if you try to impose a new 'culture' all in one fell swoop and announce at your next family gathering how unhealthy they all are and how everyone needs to change. Even if other family members know that things are grim and need to shift, they won't thank you for it.

At the same time, a culture change of some fashion needs to happen if your family get-togethers are going to be more honest and authentic. That's why a survival strategy is required that approaches changing the family get-together dynamic through manageable, incremental stages instead of trying to whip the family into shape all in one go.

Not only that, societal cultures in all parts of the world promote the idea of happy families, how important family is, how family comes first. If we look at just a few of the many phrases that have to do with family, you can see how ingrained we all are to think that family is where it's at:

- Blood is thicker than water

- *Mi casa e su casa*

- I am my brother's keeper
- The acorn doesn't fall far from the tree
- Family is where they have to take you in
- It runs in the family
- It's a family affair
- The family that prays together stays together
- Like father, like son
- Hurt me, hurt my brother
- Keep it in the family

Many of us (and many of our fellow family members as well) lug those beliefs with us when we go to our family get-togethers, and people can feel quite fierce about anyone questioning those deeply held attitudes.

All you need is love . . . or do you?

If you notice, I have hardly used the word 'love' in this book. A bit odd, that, considering this is a book about families, you might think. I've said most of us crave love from our families, and there is certainly something about the public arena of a family get-together where many of us most seek this love. We want proof of our family's feelings for us, which may or may not be given.

Much like the inferences implicit in the list of family axioms I included above, there is an implicit expectation that we will automatically love our blood relations. I've heard over and over again, 'I *have* to love him/her, he/she's my brother, sister, mother, father, aunt, uncle, cousin, niece, nephew, etc.' It is as though the tie of family is the one and only reason we should have those deep feelings.

Why? Why should we love people who are in our lives simply through an accident of birth? All of us need to ask ourselves: if I met these people as complete strangers would I want to have anything to do with them? Sometimes, the answer might be a resounding, 'Yes! I like these people; I could see myself growing to love them. We click, we get on and seem to have a lot to say to each other.' Sometimes, the answer might be a deafening, 'No! No way would I have these people in my life. No way would I put up with such appalling behaviour. No way would I have anything to do with people who think so differently and have beliefs so opposed to mine.'

In families we are expected to accept and tolerate because it's love that's important. As far as I'm concerned, love is usually the easy bit. Loving someone isn't hard to do if you have an open heart and want to connect with people. Love, however, doesn't necessarily mean healthy relationships; it doesn't mean good communication; it most certainly doesn't mean happy and pleasant family get-togethers.

Love is too often used as an excuse to justify bad behaviour: 'If you love me, you'll forgive me,' or 'I did it because I love you.' And what about that ghastly phrase: 'Love means never having to say you're sorry'? Oh, really? And that other phrase that's chucked around: 'unconditional love.' What exactly does that mean? I love you no matter what? I love you without strings? I love you just because you are? All very noble sentiments, but I think it's rare if just about non-existent to find truly unconditional love in most families. I haven't ever seen or heard about a 'stringless' family relationship; people want their love returned and if it isn't can feel devastated.

Don't get me wrong, love is grand, as they say. Being loved by your loved ones is comforting, reassuring, exhilarating. But love isn't a cure-all; it doesn't heal all wounds. It doesn't excuse thoughtlessness, humiliation, gossip, intolerance, bullying and more overt abusive behaviour. Love is a good building block for creating better family get-togethers, but it's all the rest that's going to make them healthy and strong.

You may love your sister, but if her behaviour makes being in a room with her and the rest of the family intolerable, love alone isn't going to improve things. Love may be the motivator, but it's practising adult behaviours, it's using good communication tools and it's having the will and motivation to try something new that will create a way of being with her that makes it possible for the love to flourish. It doesn't happen the other way around. If it did, very few people would have family problems because love would make everything all right. It doesn't because too many people really do think love is enough and they don't have to do anything else but love.

I gave an example earlier of a client who usually ended up in tears whenever she visited her family. If asked, she would say that her family was a very loving one. They loved each other and cared about each other. So why the tears? Why the feeling of being criticised? Why the dread of family get-togethers, knowing they generally ended in chaos? If looked at from the outside, it might appear as though love was nowhere in sight, when clearly from her perspective, they all did love one another. It was love that motivated her to try something else; love that she had for her family. However, equally important, was the love she wanted to feel when she was with them – she wanted to experience their love for her. Every time she went to a family gathering that ended up so badly, she only felt the absence of love, which made her yearning for it all that much greater.

Relationships do not get better all on their own. It takes effort, determination and skill to turn difficult relationships into more satisfying ones. Love may have something to do with it, but not everything. At family get-togethers, where there can be so many different 'players', all with their own 'agendas', love is the least of it.

Exercise four

Do you or anyone else in your family use love as an excuse?
Y/N
What behaviours get excused because of love?

Behaviour that gets excused	Who?

If you accept that love is a building block and not the answer, you can free yourself from waiting passively for it all to change just on the strength of love.

How to survive the family get-together

It's time for you to create your own strategic plan to make going to your family get-togethers less of an ordeal. I doubt you'll be able to transform really difficult family gatherings into happy ones all on your own, so the focus has to be on your behaviour and changes you need to put into place.

It means, as I pointed out right at the beginning, that your feelings may still be in as much turmoil as they ever were, but that doesn't have to stop you acting differently. It might also mean that the only thing that does change are your feelings. How do you like that for a contradiction? What I mean is that perhaps just in reading this book you will have got sufficient distance, perspective and insight into your family dynamics that you don't have to feel controlled by it all. You can know that, no matter what the situation, you always have choices. Your choice may be to stay and completely tolerate and accept others' unkind and impossible behaviour. Your choice might be to walk away. Your choice might be to find something in between, which would be about changing what you do.

A summary of what you've read so far

To help you create a viable strategy it's useful to have a summary of the main points I've included in this book:

1. Families have changed drastically in the past 50 to 70 years and thus the family get-together has changed as well.

2. Most families have a far greater 'cocktail mix' than ever before. The more complex the mix, the more potentially volatile or difficult the family get-together.

3. Family dynamics are either moving forward and developing or moving in a perpetual loop which keeps things stuck.

4. Not only do other family members get up your nose, but you, too, get up other people's noses in the same way.

5. Most people have fantasies about how they wish their family would behave, or have expectations that it's all going to be dreadful.

6. It's hard to be your authentic self if you are pretending or stuck in wishful thinking, or if you are expecting torments.

7. It's hard to be your authentic self if you feel you are entering alien territory when you go to family gatherings, or the family gathering is at yours.

8. Family 'sculpting' can help you step back and see your family with a bit of distance.

9. Just about everyone (except in very, very rare exceptions) has good qualities. Your strong feelings about someone will colour whether you can recognise and acknowledge their positive traits, especially if you always view them negatively.

10. Fantasy Mind Maps can help you get at the heart of some of the issues that bother you at family events. You can redraw a Fantasy Mind Map to see situations from a different perspective.

11. You will have knee-jerk reactions to certain people in your family, and the things they do and say.

12. Everyone to a greater or lesser degree plays out unhelpful and difficult behaviour. It is good for you to recognise which you do.

13. Everyone has roles that they play at family get-togethers. First, you need to be aware of the roles you play. Then you can consciously change your roles in order to change the family dynamics.

14. Every family has rules (spoken and unspoken) and patterns that get played out when people are together. Changing rules and patterns will also change the family dynamics.

15. It's useful to identify any popcorn statements you and others in your family use when you are all together.

16. Point scoring is common in families and you will feel vulnerable in certain situations so it's easy to get 'got'.

17. Charting a family-o-gram could be a useful way to identify some of the patterns, roles and rules that get played out in your family, and perhaps have been playing out for a number of generations.

18. Family patterns will often get played out amongst other groups outside the family.

19. Unconsciously, you may already be passing some of the less appetising family patterns on to your own children.

20. It's 'normal' to be resistant to change.

21. It's seductive for family members to live in their memories and use them as currency or weapons to get at other people and perpetuate hard feelings.

22. Listening to how other family members have experienced the same event can help you gain additional insight and perspective on family dynamics and on memory.

23. One of the greatest skills you can hone is the ability to see situations from other people's points of view ('walk a mile in someone else's shoes').

24. Listening with empathy goes hand in hand with seeing things from someone else's perspective.

25. Forgiving others usually means that, first, you need to forgive yourself.

26. Holding on to grudges is harmful to your health; being aware of why you find it hard to let go of them will at least gain you some personal awareness.

27. When you were very young you didn't have too many choices in what happened to you. Families often unconsciously undermine their children's self-confidence and self-esteem, which follows them right into adulthood.

28. All the while you behave immaturely, you will probably be treated immaturely by your family. You will most likely have an 'age' where some of your behaviour got stuck, usually for a very good reason.

29. You will most likely have an experience of either pretending to be someone you're not, and/or pretending that everything is just fine in the family when it's not.

30. It is essential to remember the distinction between childish behaviour and childlike behaviour. Childlike can be good.

31. Practising adult behaviour is one of the most challenging and ultimately freeing things you can do to make your family get-togethers better.

32. Most people, understandably, will have a number of big fears when thinking about changing their own behaviour within the family.

33. Being aware of what fears motivate you (or should that be *de*motivate?) will help you free yourself from them.

34. Big holidays and other big events often bring out the worst in families. Dramas and other crises get announced or played out at these gatherings more than usual.

35. In many families, emotional and psychological, as well as physical, boundaries are often blurred. Learning to set boundaries is another essential skill if you want to have happier get-togethers.

36. It's easy for families to get distracted by little stuff in order to hide from or cover up the bigger issues.

37. Unhealthy families need a 'culture change' if they are going to thrive.

38. Love isn't enough.

39. Heavenly families have just as many issues, problems and difficulties as hellish ones, but they have a willingness, desire and ability to resolve their difficulties.

40. You always have a choice.

Personal survival strategy

Step one: Identify any awarenesses, insights and new perspectives – large or small – that you have had about your family and your family get-togethers.

____

____

____

____

____

Step two: Identify any of your own behaviour that you believe contributes to some of the less than happy family get-togethers you attend.

Step three: List any fears you may have identified in Chapter Eight that would stop you from changing your own behaviour at your family get-togethers.

How realistic are those fears?

Step four: Identify and list any exercises, techniques, adult behaviours, options or suggestions I've included in this book that you think fit your personality and that, if you haven't tried them already, you would find manageable.

Step five: Choose the easiest upcoming family get-together and decide, *ahead of time*, on whom you will practise these new behaviours. It's alright to plan the opening gambit of any conversations you expect to have, as long as you don't fall into the trap of making up what they might say in response – because you just don't know.

If you think it will be easier, you can single out one or two family members on whom to practise outside the get-together 'stage'.

If at all possible 'enlist' other family members you think might support your attempts at changing the family dynamics.

Step six: Accept that things may not (and probably will not) change overnight. If you don't notice anything changing, plan what you could do differently at the next event, and the next one and the next one after that. You may feel as though nothing is happening, but if you continue to change, it will have an effect on the family get-together.

____

____

____

____

____

Step seven: Celebrate any success with a trusted friend. Then keep right on practising at every opportunity you get.

A strategy is one of those things that should never be written in stone. It needs to be flexible and responsive to whatever comes back at you. The more you understand yourself and are aware of the complexities of your family dynamics, the more you will be able to adjust and refine your survival strategy with each family get-together.

It's OK

Here's another bit of advice: be assured that no one can practise heavenly adult behaviour *all* the time. No one can always think of the perfect thing to say or the ideal behaviour to display. I sure as hell can't be conscious all the time, and without thinking I can get hooked into actions I'd rather have avoided. But it's OK. It's OK to fall into your roles without thinking, or follow your rules and family patterns when you aren't looking.

You know how sometimes it's great to go to the cinema and eat a giant tub of popcorn? It has minimal nutritional value, but it sure tastes good going down. In the same way, every once in a while it's OK to splurge in a mini-orgy of popcorn statements. It won't be of much benefit to anybody but it sure may feel good when you're doing it. The key, of course, is to realise, even if after the fact, that that is what you've done; had a bit of a self-indulgent popcorn moment.

It's OK to wish 'they' were different every once in a while and indulge in some Fantasyland thinking.

It's OK to want to throttle one or two of your family members, and it's OK to want to shout at them all to, 'Just shut up, will you!'

Any of this is OK, as long as you don't do it too much and for too long, which would mean you're just back in the same old patterns.

Top ten survival tips

On top of all that I have my personal top ten tips for surviving the family get-together. You may have identified others that you may find useful to keep in mind; I know that these hold me in good stead – when I remember to remember them:

1. See reality for what it is, not what you hope it's going to be.

   This requires that you put aside wishful thinking and recognise your family for who they are, not who you fantasise they could be. Seeing reality not only means avoiding wishful thinking, but it also means acknowledging some of the more positive qualities of your most difficult family members.

2. Be prepared.

   Knowing who your family is means you can prepare your strategy ahead of time (as in the survival strategy above) so that you aren't continually disappointed or frustrated. This goes hand in hand with seeing reality because in order to be prepared you have to be able to see clearly what it is you are preparing for.

3. Make your intentions clear and set boundaries for other people.

   These rub shoulders with each other. People aren't going to read your mind, so you have to let them know what your plans are. If you plan to stay a short while, then announce that beforehand or just when you arrive; if you want to go away for Christmas and not spend it with the family, you have to let them know in time for them to adjust. And so on.

Be very clear what you expect from others as well as how far you are willing to go. Boundary setting is a way of avoiding operating out of the extremes of 'I have to put up with it' or 'I just won't go'.

4. Avoid trying to control the situation.

   When you have a picture of how you think other people ought to behave, it's easy to fall into controlling, even borderline bullying behaviour as you try to get them to be how you want them to be.

   Once you learn to let go of your need to control others, some of your family get-togethers might actually be more relaxing. This, of course, leads to my next tip . . .

5. Let the other person be another person as long as they aren't harming you or others.

   One of my mantras is about allowing other people to be their quirky, strange and individual selves.

6. Step outside the arena when things start hotting up.

   'When the going gets tough, the tough get going' is a favourite maxim of some people. My version is 'when the going gets tough, get yourself outta there'. Even if it's for a few minutes, go make a cup of tea, go to the toilet, go for a walk, but get yourself out of the line of fire if at all possible. This is sort of the equivalent of counting to ten and will give you a chance to cool off, or give you some think time so you can decide the best way to resolve the situation.

7. Know your bottom line.

   Although finding a resolution to family get-together difficulties is always the ideal option, it quite simply isn't possible all the time. You need to decide what your bottom line is: the behaviour you absolutely won't tolerate, the shenanigans you won't put up with, the words you won't accept directed at you. If you determine your bottom line before you go to a family get-together, you can practise some of the other top tips rather than fall into knee-jerk reactions.

8. Let them be 'right'.

   Sometimes it's a good idea to just let other people be right. Avoid the fight, concede, be gracious. As long as it isn't habitual (anything for a peaceful life, remember?), then giving in gracefully can create generous feelings in other people.

9. Accept that you may have a good enough family which has good enough family get-togethers.

   The good enough family. This requires you to accept that you do not and never will have an ideal family. That your family may have some trying and extremely difficult members in it, that they are frustrating and make you angry at times. However, when you can focus more on people's good and caring qualities, it can be easier to see that though you don't have a truly heavenly family, yours is good enough to hang in there with.

10. You always have a choice.

    Though it may feel it at times, once you reach adulthood, your family doesn't really control you; you are in charge of your own destiny. No matter how dire the situation or how wonderful, you have the power to choose what you do and with whom you do it. You may feel

> manipulated, bullied, humiliated, but the choice is always there to do something about it.
>
> I'm certainly not saying it's always easy to be master of your own destiny, given the sometimes inexorable pressure families bring to bear. However, decisions about what *you* do with *yourself* lie with you.

The key importance with tips is to remember them and practise them.

The family get-together, be it a wedding, funeral, anniversary party, birthday bash or Sunday lunch, can be a whole lot more enjoyable when you enter into them in a spirit of staying in charge of your own behaviours instead of being buffeted by old and stuck patterns.

Feelings finale

I said at the beginning your feelings are just that – feelings. You can change what you do and what you say without having to change how you feel. I wonder if you feel any differently about your family than you did at the start of this survival guide, and if so, what has changed?

It's all right if nothing has changed. Your feelings might be exactly the same. It's how you conduct yourself at future family get-togethers that is important.

However, I do have one final exercise. I'd like you to identify your most heavenly behaviour, what makes you a special family member and how you contribute to having healthier, happier family get-togethers.

See you on Cloud Nine.

About the Author

Jo Ellen Grzyb is a keen, passionate and devoted gardener who also happens to be a writer and co-founder/Director of Impact Factory, a training and personal development company specialising in making work a better place to be.

Jo Ellen, who holds dual American and British Citizenship, spent 20 years in the arts, entertainment and corporate sectors in development work on both sides of the Atlantic before setting up Impact Factory with Robin Chandler in 1991.

She trained as a counsellor/psychotherapist and is particularly interested in facilitating people so they can fulfil their dreams and aspirations while keeping an eye firmly on reality. However, it is now through her writing that she most touches people.

Childfree and Loving It!
Nicki Defago

> 'The responsibility of parenthood is overwhelming and incredibly stressful. And it's for life. Don't give up a pleasant life, for a life of unpaid drudgery. Your standard of living drastically declines, and the kids take off as soon as they can, without a backward glance.'
>
> Shirley Conran

We live in a child-centred society. Women, no matter how high achieving in other areas, are pitied and patronised if they are childless, and condemned as selfish if this is by choice. However large numbers of women are enjoying their hard-won independence, and are reluctant to give it all up to become slaves to their children. And many men feel the same way.

Childfree and Loving It! is a broad, definitive exploration of non-parenthood, challenging the myths of parenthood and boldly proclaiming the joys of a childfree life. Nicki Defago explores population growth and the environment, workplace policies and consumerism, and interviews those who have chosen not to have children as well as the honest parents who wish they hadn't.

If you have ever questioned the need for children or sighed with relief that you don't have any – then this is the book for you.

Non-fiction: Sociology/Parenting
1-904132-63-4
UK: £10.99
US: $17.95
www.fusionpress.co.uk